Forest Dawn

Reflections of the
Rising Light

Michael Forester

First published in Great Britain in 2020
by Paralight Press

www.michaelforester.co.uk

The right of Michael Forester
to be identified as author of this work
has been asserted by him in accordance with
the Copyright, Designs and Patents Act 1988

ISBN: 978-1-8380114-0-6

Cover Design by BookBeaver
Cover Image © Mark Aldworth, reproduced with kind
permission

PARALIGHT

PRESS

When a stranger approaches, and we think he is our brother, and all conflicts disappear, that is the moment when night ends and day begins.

Shimon Peres,
as quoted by Paulo Coelho in
Like The Flowing River

Reader Feedback for *Forest Rain*, the preceding book to *Forest Dawn*:

Nothing seems more important than my swift response to receiving Forest Rain through the post. Thank you for writing it. I feel so honoured to have a copy. I am halfway through reading it and I cannot put it down. My soul is responding, knowing that this is one of the great books of all time.

Katherine, UK

I'm reading Forest Rain (couldn't sleep) – undergoing a very emotional healing as I weep for my mother, my family, myself, lost love, missed opportunities.

Caroline, UK.

This is not a book like any other I have read. Mankind has been looking for this message for a very long time. I urge you to clear your mind. Turn your phone off, turn the television off, turn the radio off. Change into your most comfortable clothes, grab a box of tissues, and get comfortable in your favorite reading space. As you read Forest Rain, listen not only to Michael's words, but pay attention to the emotions and self-examination you experience. Soon, you will start to see beyond Michael's experiences, and you will start to see your own.

Ann, California

A wonderful read! There are a lot of life lessons to be learned from the different stories in this book. I would recommend this to anyone who's on a journey of finding their soul!

Rachel, UK

Forest Rain simply touched the recesses of my soul. I could not help but shed tears as I pondered upon each word, each line, each paragraph and the whole of the essays and so with every word, every line, every stanza of each of the poems. I could not even refrain from rereading it the nth time. And each time I do, the effect would be the same.

Janet Pascual, Philippines

Reading Forest Rain allowed myself to re-evaluate my current position in life and to seek peace with the flaws that I have yet to forgive myself for. The book is beautifully written, with many insights and valuable lessons that readers can carry with them in their everyday life. For someone who seeks to find clarity, peace and understanding, I would highly recommend Forest Rain, for your heart will be touched and you will learn to flourish in the journey that awaits you. The books serves as a brilliant inspiration for those who seek to mend their souls and find peace with oneself.

Sarah Soon, Philippines

…and the next thing I knew, I was falling at the deepest pit of this book that made it so hard for me to put it down. As I was reading this book, I'm not that aware on how the author himself touches my soul, like what he had mentioned in the first part of this book. I just realized it the moment I felt my own tears drenching my cheeks.

Janel Ranola, Philippines

I would ask yourself the question "Can you love yourself at this time in this life?" This book will give you a deep understanding of yourself and self-realisation of your worth to others.

Susan Aldworth, UK

If you care about the world, you need to read this book. It will open doors in your heart and mind.

Di, UK

I feel like I was meant to read this book. I cannot put it down. I feel like somebody is looking out for me and knew I should find this book. It is the kind of book you need to hold on to as it is relevant in everybody's lives.

Remarla, UK

Forest Rain is riddled with excellent writing, beautifully communicated and luxuriously gift-wrapped for our senses. The author is inviting us deeper into his own personal world, opening up doors that few writers would dare to reveal. We start page one as a stranger and become a trusted friend long before the final line is done This book is an absolute gem and I feel honoured to have read it. I sincerely wish that I'd written it.

Kev, UK

By reading Forest Rain, I finally answered the question "Who am I?"

Karl, Philippines

I could not help but ponder upon every word, paragraph, chapter of the whole book. Through this spiritual book you can discover the astounding, deep and profound messages that signify to you alone.

Emily, Philippines

Forest Rain has washed me deep with its radiance and

beauty. It is rejuvenating and life-giving. I read it for the second time and each time the journey inward has been illuminating and profound. Such is the beauty of the writer's expressions that once we immerse into its depth we can't leave it until we experience the entire journey revealed so beautifully.

Sangeeta, Assam, India

Contents

Introduction

You're walking in the Forest at dawn.
There was rain in the night – a deluge.
Along your path are many pools left by the downpour.
As the sun comes up, light is pouring through the trees,
reflecting on the pools.
Ahead of you, a stranger is walking.
You walk faster to catch them up.
As you approach, the person ahead of you stops, turns, and look
into your eyes.
At first, you're embarrassed.
The directness is too much; until you own it.
And then, you understand.
The eyes you are looking into, are your own.

Who is this stranger you encounter when you look into a pool of still water; the one whose face you recognise but whose soul is deeper than you knew? She is the person who speaks to you from the silent place, when you have forsaken all the other voices that clamour for your attention. If the time has come for you to listen to him, he will tell you all you need to know about this journey you have chosen to call your life; the purpose of the painful and the shame of the senseless that happened long ago, the meaning that lies around you on the path now, the light that is yet to come.

Reach out to what is inside. Reach in to what is outside. Drink deep from that pool whenever you will. And when you do, take hold of what you find and wrestle with it until the dawn comes. For when it does, though you may be forever marked in the hollow of your thigh, you will reflect the light, the light that always shined inside.

1. A Pound of Peace

"A pound of Peace, please, mate," said the man in front of me in the queue at the market stall. His shopping bag was packed full and I wondered how he was going to fit any more into it.

"Beautiful bit of Peace, this is," the stallholder commented, weighing out a pound on the scales. "You'll not find better in the market today."

The customer smiled his thanks and pressed the Peace down onto his bag that was already bulging with Worry, Regret and Frustration. It looked precariously balanced as he walked away. I wasn't surprised to see it topple out and splatter into the gutter.

"And what can I do for you today, sir?" The stallholder's voice brought my attention back to the table. "How about some Pleasure for your supper? Just sprinkle a bit of Indolence on it and fry it in Indulgence – beautiful!"

Tempted, I checked my wallet. "Sorry," I replied, "I'm all out of Trust to pay you with."

"That don't matter," he retorted, "I take all the major cards – Gullibility, Foolishness, Ignorance. And if you've got that new one, Complacency, I can even give you a discount." He winked at me. "In fact, some of my customers just transfer what they owe on their cards month to month. You can buy with Gullibility today, then move the debt to your Foolishness at the end of the month. That way, you never have to pay for anything, really."

My eye was caught by an empty box in the middle of the table, marked 'Happiness'. "What's happened to that one?"

"Happiness? Oh, that's long gone. If you want Happiness you have to get here when I open. People sometimes queue overnight for Happiness. An' they buy as much of it as they can carry, on account of the fact that it doesn't last very long."

I was disappointed. "Have you got any Contentment then?" I asked.

"Contentment? Bless me! I ain't been asked for Contentment since I can't remember when. It's long gone out of fashion." Then, his voice dropped. "Tell you what," he said, "What you need is this." He looked about to make sure no one was watching, then slid a little box across the table to me.

"What is it?" I asked, my eyes widening.

He paused, and leaned over to whisper in my ear. "Gratification," he said, looking a bit smug. "Only – it's black market, init? So, keep it to yerself. Take this and in ten minutes I guarantee nothing will worry you again – ever."

I pulled back, feeling threatened. "So, what's that?" I asked, nodding towards a rather sickly looking plant at the end of the table.

"That? Oh, that's Love. Don't get much call for Love now. It used to be popular years ago, but it's hard work, see, and no one's willing to take the trouble with it any more. It has to be home-reared in a well mulched soil of Tenderness and watered every day with a warm solution of Kindness and Commitment. If you've got the patience, it will grow into a strong tree. But most folk are too busy to grow Love these days. You can have this one for nothing if you want. I'm not likely to sell it before it dies, now."

I liked the idea of growing my very own Love. But I didn't know if it I was willing to make the effort. So, I took the

Gratification instead. It was really expensive and took me right up to my limit on all my cards.

"Got the time?" I asked the stallholder as I turned to walk away.

"Five minutes to midnight," he answered, without even looking at his watch.

"Thanks," I said, stepping over the Peace that lay discarded in the gutter. "I'll be back for some Happiness first thing in the morning. I might even take that Love."

He smiled at me. But he knew I wouldn't.

2. I Dreamed a Dream

I dreamed a dream and in my dream I stood upon the Plain of Desolation. Upon this plain, towards me came a column of men that stretched back, far into the Mountains of Despair.

First, there came the bully, who, in childhood, supressed his pain with the short-lived glee that he found in ransacking my self-confidence. Weeping, he beseeched me, saying, "I have learned how wrong I was and I am so, so sorry. Will you forgive me?" Deep, I dipped into the wells of anguish to draw up incandescent rage, until, in manufactured indignation, I declared, "Be gone, my persecutor! You, who stole my school days, miring me in misery. You will find no forgiveness here." He turned, head bowed, and walked away.

And then, I felt much better, for a while.

In my dream.

There, closely followed my abuser, the one who commandeered my body for his pleasure, soiling my self-worth until I believed that I was vile, unlovable, unclean.

Weeping, he beseeched me, saying, "I have learned how wrong I was and I am so, so sorry. Will you forgive me?" Silently, my cries of misery relived the endless nights when he would come to steal me from myself. I supressed my tears and would not let him see his handiwork, carved deep, indelible upon my heart. I turned my face away from him and drew some satisfaction by denying him the forgiveness that he sought. He turned, head bowed, and walked away.

And then, I felt much better, for a while.

In my dream.

Next, before me stood my torturer – the one who had ripped fingernails and hope from me, until I screamed in terror at his shadow, cast upon my dungeon wall. For when he was done with torture and all my hope had fled, I betrayed my comrades, naming them, one by one. Weeping, he beseeched me, saying, "I have learned how wrong I was and I am so, so sorry. Will you forgive me?" Words of revulsion stuck in my throat as I remembered his indifferent contempt. A violent anger rose within me and I struck him on the cheek and spat into his eyes. He turned, head bowed, and walked away.

And then, I felt much better, for a while.

In my dream.

All day, the line moved on, men who were my persecutors, shuffling back across the years to stand before me, each seeking my forgiveness. Each, in their turn, I rejected, until, with shoulders hunched and eyes cast down to earth, they slunk away to meditate upon their monstrous deeds.

As the sun sank low towards the mountains, there came the perpetrators of great crimes. Attila, Genghis Khan, Pol Pot, Peter Sutcliffe, Harold Shipman and many, many more I did not know by name. Each man sought the same: to find a place of absolution, a gentle touch, a word to sooth their aguish for their wrongs. Until at last there stood before me, Adolf Hitler, who looked into my eyes. "You too?" I asked.

From each one came the words, "I have learned how wrong I was and I am so, so sorry. Will you forgive me?"

None would I forgive, for none deserved forgiveness.

In my dream.

And at the last, just as the sun fell upon the mountains, its final rays casting blood-light on the plain, there came to me the great deceiver, Satan, weeping on his knees. He would not lift his head, but falling on my feet beseeched me, saying, "I am so, so sorry for all the evil I have wrought, on angels, worlds, and all the peoples of the Earth. I tell you, my repentance is true and utter. And though I do not deserve it, I dare to wonder, is there any hope that you could find forgiveness in your heart for me, the greatest wrongdoer of them all?"

I spoke my verdict in an instant. "Not now, not ever, not for you, nor any of your children, for I have not finished hating you."

In my dream I turned around and looked at God. "Let me know when you have," said God, "for there is so much love I am waiting to give you."

3. Treading on Spiders

Picture if you will, a boy of eight walking down the High Street in his home town in a north London suburb. He is dressed in a red school cap, a knee-length coat, underneath which he is wearing short grey trousers (he hates these; he is desperate to graduate to long trousers). His gaze is fixed down on the pavement in front of him whilst, hand-in-hand with his father, he is being led forward towards some unknown and not very interesting destination. His attention is distracted by a large, long-legged spider on the pavement, just within reach of his foot. He makes one of those split-second, semi-conscious decisions and, in the way of eight-year-old boys, stamps on it, more from the interest of seeing it flattened than in malice. But his aim is off centre. He hits the spider with the sole of his black, lace-up shoe, but not firmly enough to kill it. Instead, as he glances back, still moving forward at his father's hurried pace, he sees it semi-squashed on the paving stone, still kicking in anguish with two of its legs that remained uncrushed. At that moment, an awareness flashes into his mind that this creature has been alive; alive in some way that was comparable to his own state of being alive. And he is conscious that he has all but ended its life. It will now expire in some version of pain known to insects, which, in his eight-year-old mind, is wholly comparable to the pain he knows he is capable of feeling. Any pleasure he might have taken in the experience of treading on the spider has drained rapidly away. He is chastened. He feels self-induced shame for perhaps the first time in his life.

I don't think I ever repeated that act, and even now, I go to great lengths to avoid killing anything that lives.

At that moment, the awareness had dawned, as it does for all of us, eventually, that physical life will one day end. Yet, when we first gain a realisation of impermanence, it is usually dissociated. The life of a spider, a foreigner, an elderly distant relative may be finite, but my life is infinite. As long as I can remember, I have existed. Therefore, I will always be.

Then, of course, as it was always meant to, something changes. We are stopped short by a reframe of our unconscious beliefs that is so powerful as to be able to shake our faith in the most basic tenets of our assurance of our own identity: we have mortality thrust upon us. Commonly, it comes at the death of someone or something with whom we have an emotional bond. Death, that audacious thief, breaks through an unlatched window into our certainty, or hammers down a door we had bolted to preserve the immortality of some dearly beloved family member. He ransacks our confidence. He rifles through the musty draws of sentiment in which we have long stored the jewels of our faith in confused chaotic jumbles. Then, he makes away with the sparkling jewels of certainty with which we have adorned our ignorance.

It is then, in the harsh daylight of uncompromising awareness, that we come to understand that the actual or impending death of someone we love dearly redefines them as mortal; finite; a being with a beginning and an end and a fistful of lessons learned in between. Then it is that we weep for the death of immortality. We grieve for the realisation that our dear one's humanity is finite and their flesh like grass. We are tempted to pretend it is not going to happen. If we are willing to face it at all, we wish we could spare them the experience. All the while, we fail to understand that death and the process of dying is amongst the most important of lessons that we have come here to learn. Were we able to prevent that loved one's impending death, we would rob them of their final lesson as surely as that thief robbed us of our ignorance.

As if all this were not enough, we also find that the thief has made away with something else equally, or perhaps even more precious. We are devastated to find that our own immortality has been wrested away from our unconscious grasp. The question that we then face is perhaps the most important that we ever have, or ever will address. The coming of the question marks the disappearance of the last vestiges of childhood and the final arrival of pre-maturity. Our answer to it defines how we will live the truly adult portion of our lives which proves to be a much, much smaller part of the total than we ever imagined it could be. And the question itself? Simply this: in the light of our awareness that this physical life is not forever, what will we choose to do with the remaining time that we have? Will we squander it in the haphazard pursuit of a lost immature ignorance, a happy-ever-after fairy tale that can never be regained? Will we shop 'til we drop for Prada handbags to buttress our uneasy sense of self-worth? Will we storm political heights of infamy? Will we hunger for Hollywood-perpetuated myths of satisfaction and power that material wealth and positions of control purportedly bestow? Will we eat, drink and be mesmerised in the certainty that tomorrow we die? Or will we, perhaps, rise to the glory of ascendant awareness where tongues of flame will seat themselves upon our brow?

If it is to be the last of these, perhaps we can finally say with some confidence that we have reached the end of the beginning of our journey. We can embrace our impermanence and discover we are capable of looking out beyond the dilapidated boundaries of our souls to a place where we can do more than see through a glass darkly; where we can begin to see face to face.

We are all confronted with this choice at one time or another. We all have the right to make it for ourselves and there is no one with the legitimate entitlement to criticise the choices that another makes regarding the pace of their spiritual growth. But when the party mask of fleshly immortality is cast off and we are confronted with the finite time we are allotted in this life, there is a call ... a requirement ... a summons that each and every one of us must answer before moving forward in our chosen direction, be it growth, be it aggrandisement or be it indolence:

"Choose you this day whom you will serve."

4. Taking Refuge

Here ends the life of a victim
washed up on an English seashore.
Placed two million and nine
he stood in a line
and behind him stood two million more.

He had run through the ruins of Mosul.
With his wife from Aleppo they fled.
Through minefields and shell holes
and barefoot through hell holes,
the feet of his baby, they bled.

They crawled through the mud in the darkness,
in nakedness, hunger and pain.
With his child on his back
he ducked from the flak
but for her he would do it again.

And I watched on my screen at the horror
while Hungarians I thought like me
strung barbed wire in fences
and called it defences
then laughed in hysterical glee.

He walked two thousand miles across Europe,
his wife and his child by his side,
'til they fell down exhausted
and there were accosted.
His daughter just lay down and died.

His wife rocked the dead child in mourning
while the thieves stole the pennies they'd scraped.
In his hunger and thirst
he struggled and cursed,
held down while he watched his wife raped.

They stood in the camp near to Calais.
The danger they tried to ignore,
while they got in a boat
too leaky to float –
you do that when fleeing from war.

The boat, it went down halfway over.
All forty-eight souls, they were lost
in a craft built for ten
– save for two wealthy men
who counted the cash not the cost.

Come not to my nation, you hopeful.
Though Jesus, it's said that he saves,
Dave said "Five thousand in –
any more is a sin
and Britannia, she still rules the waves."

Your suffering no longer moves us.

And the sea, well your body it bloats.
For in sheer desperation
the soul of my nation
was sold for a handful of votes.

You're dirty and smelly and foreign.
Your skin's not the colour of mine.
So I'll play on my iPhone
while I cast the first stone –
Be off with you – Get back in line.

We're tired of watching you suffer.
It's late and we're heading for bed.
Were those your last screams?
Then get off of our screens –
We're relieved that you're finally dead.

5. Entertaining Angels

Does God have a sense of humour?

You may think there are more important matters to consider in a world of turmoil and uncertainty. I'm not so sure.

Yesterday, I visited an apartment about to be rented out. I wanted to make sure I was giving them the correct set of keys (Wot me? Give someone the wrong keys? Er, it has been known...)

So, I'm checking the flat over and all is well and, yes, the keys do actually fit the locks. I head back to the ground floor whistling a happy tune and think, 'Oh yes, better try the key to the bin room door and the garage.' I insert the key into the bin room door. It turns. It opens. I smile. So you know what's coming now, don't you?... Off to the garage I go and insert the key into the lock. All is well. I turn the key. It turns. It opens. I smile. I remember thinking at that point, 'I'll leave the bunch of keys in the lock – I'm only going to be here a second.' I turn the handle slowly (the new tenant's been storing possessions in the garage prior to moving in and I don't know what's in there). Then woosh! The garage door heads skyward at a velocity that would not have disgraced a self-respecting Soyuz space rocket.

A quick visual check tells me the tenant is using the garage as agreed, so, now to close the door and retrieve my keys. Only, er, no. As I pull down on the door, one side starts to come down.

The other doesn't budge. I pull a little harder. Only a little harder you understand. I'm not stoopid ya know. I can see that if I pull too hard I'll end up warping the door. So, it still doesn't move. I stand back and look at it. It still doesn't move (funny, that). I go inside the garage and look at the door from behind. And now, I can see the business end of an up-and-over garage door; all wires and pulleys and handles and ratchets and snugworsticating splanges (if you don't know what one of those is, shame on you. Every self-respecting handyman should have a snugworsticating splange doer-upper in his toolbox). Ok, I admit it. I'm no engineer. But this is a garage door, right? Not Virgin Galactica, right? So, yours truly should be able to make sense of it, right?

Wrong.

Thirty minutes later, I'm still standing by the door, looking at it from the inside and the outside and it's still not closing (funny, that). And then, I see why. On the right hand side of the door, looking out, is a wire (that's me doing the looking out, not the wire, you understand). The wire has a thingy attached to the end of it. The thingy isn't doing anything. Now, although I must confess I'm not an engineer, I know enough about business economics to conclude that the average designer of garage doors isn't going to design a wire to hang loosely by the side of the door doing nothing just so engineeringly challenged individuals like me can admire it when confronted by a door's refusal to close. The problem is the loose wire. Definitely. It's errr... loose. So I look for where it might attach. And then a revelation of Archimedean proportions hits me. If I look on the other side of the door, there might be another wire. And if that one's still attached, I'll see what I'm supposed to do with the loose wire to make the door work! And oh, thank you, angels. There is indeed a wire on the other side. And it is indeed still attached. I can't rightly say why both wires need to be attached in the same way, but my post-renaissance sense of symmetry tells me that they should. Definitely. Probably. Maybe. Heyyy! There's nothing to this garage door engineering business, is there? Moi is a world-class broken garage door fixer. All I now have to do is reattach the loose wire on the right-hand side of the door to its snugworsticating splange just like wot the one on the left-hand side is, then all will be well. And then, I can go home and have a nice cuppa tea. Which is just as well, cos it's coming to rain. So, I reattach the wire. And I'm ready to go home for the cuppa, right? Yeah. Except, the wire comes off again.

I reattach it.

It comes off a second time.

I fold my arms, put my head on one side and think about it.

Nothing happens (funny, that).

So, there's nothing for it but to text the company that installed the door (don't you just hate admitting defeat?). Only I don't have my phone. It's at home with my hearing dog, Matt, having a nice cuppa tea (how very sensible of both of them). And I'm here without it. And it's raining. And if I go home to get it there might be armies of brigands round the corner just salivating at the prospect of plundering an unattended garage whose up-and-over door won't close and which is full of second-hand furniture the sale of which will make them rich beyond their wildest dreams of avarice.

No, I didn't buy that one either.

So, I run round the corner in the rain to collect my phone and get drenched in the process. As I enter the door, Matt eyes me disdainfully. So does the phone. I pick up the phone. And the brolly. Cos I'm not gonna get wet twice. I'm not stoopid, ya know. Only, when I get outside the rain has stopped. So, I rush back, certain the brigand army will be hard at work removing my tenant's possessions. Only, when I get back there's no one there (funny, that).

So, I text the installation company and wait. And I wait. And no one texts back, so I text again. And I wait. And I wait. And I really don't know what to do now. So, what would you do?

I know what you'd do. You'd pray, wouldn't you?

So, I pray. Which is probably what I should have done in the first place. At least, I ask my angels for a practical solution to this problem. And I wait. And I fold my arms looking at the door again. And nothing happens (funny, that). Until ten minutes or so later, slowly past the garage comes one of those enormous pick-up truck type vehicles that look like liquid aggression on four wheels. Big, shiny, black, imposing, with a large covered flatbed on the back for the storage of whatever. And in the cab, is a man who looks like he's big and looks like he's probably got long hair an' lots of tattoos an' earrings an' stuff and eats non-engineering whimps like me for elevenses. He looks at me enquiringly as he goes past. And I put on my most helpless most appealing please-help-me look. And as he makes a three-point-turn, I pluck up enough courage to walk over.

And the big guy with the long hair an' the tattoos an' earrings an' stuff, winds down the window and says "Godda problem?"

And then, he smiles; a really kind smile. Big guys with long hair an' tattoos an' earrings an' stuff aren't supposed to smile much. And when they do, it's supposed to be a leery, grimacy, nasty kind of smile; cos they're supposed to eat whimps like me for elevenses. But right now, I really need that smile more than anything in the world. Well, maybe not more than I need a snugworsticating splange doer-upper, but you get my drift.

And I say rather sheepishly, "My garage door won't close."

And the big guy with the long hair an' the tattoos an' the earrings an' stuff says, "Has the zigglydebogaldybok wire come loose?" (Go easy on me guys, I'm deaf, ya know. I didn't quite get exactly what he said.)

And I say, "Yeah, I think it did."

And he says, "What you need is a snugworsticating splange doer-upper."

And I say, "Yeah, I know. Have you got one?"

And the big guy with the long hair an' the tattoos an' the earrings an' stuff says, "Yup. In the back. I used to be a garage door installer, but now, I'm a fireman." And I didn't ask why he still had his garage door installation tools still in the back, now he was a fireman, cos that really would have amounted to a close dental examination of an unrecompensed equine, wouldn't it?

So, the big guy with the long hair an' the tattoos an' earrings an' stuff who used to be a garage door installer but now is a fireman, gets out of the big, shiny, black, imposing pick-up truck and goes to the flatbed and takes out his snugworsticating splange doer-upper. And he smiles at me again and he fixes my zigglydebogaldybok wire.

And he won't take any payment. He just smiles from earring to earring and drives off.

And I realise that I've never seen him before. And there was no obvious reason why he should have been where he was just at the moment when I really, really needed him. And somehow, I don't think I'll be seeing him again in this lifetime.

So, I go home and make a cuppa tea. And as I'm sitting drinking it and giving Matt a cuddle, the phone vibrates with a text from the installation company asking how they can help.

And I think about a bible verse – Hebrews 13.2: Be not forgetful to entertain strangers: for thereby some have entertained angels unawares.

Yeah, God's got a sense of humour. Definitely. Funny, that.

6. Return of the Shadow Man

I wake with a picture in my mind. It takes a moment to realise it's the old dismantled Brockenhurst to Ringwood railway line at Longslade Bottom. This is the first morning following an operation to receive a cochlear implant on which I have felt fit enough to take a decent walk. I am filled with the urge to walk the old railway line. So, we take the car and head down to the Longslade Bottom car park. It has to be ten years since we last walked here. Matt doesn't remember. He's not bothered. He leaps out of the car like the three-year-old he thinks he still is and dashes off to chase rabbits he will never catch into the rising sun. I follow in subservient compliance.

All life, it seems, will now be divided into the periods of BI and AI, before the implant and after the implant, my personal parody of the Gregorian calendar. I can already tell that it is different out here since the last time we walked the Forest, BI. The sun is lower in the sky, and the shadows are a little longer. Even I can feel the silence here. Nevertheless, it is later in the morning than we usually walk and we do not have the Forest to ourselves as we normally consider ourselves entitled to.

Nature is becoming lazier. She has started her inexorable countdown to Autumn. Though the leaves are still copious on the trees, the heather is beginning to carpet the floor in purple. It will intensify these next two weeks or so, until it screams for your attention from every hillside. Today, it whispers quietly. It is asking me if I am using the summer well.

That question seems a little unfair. 'I've been convalescing,' I want to tell her. I'm not expected to do much. But she is insistent. So, quietly, I enumerate the various tasks I have been undertaking: promoting this book, preparing that one for publication, revising another ready for release next year. Yes, I think I have used the summer well. But then, I realise: she is talking about writing.

We pass a small group of Highland Longhorn cattle. They look strangely green in the waning summer sunlight. I am relieved they show no inclination to chase Matt. He is old now, and despite his self-delusion, I doubt he could outrun them for long.

We have been walking parallel to the railway line but I see he is beginning to slow with the rest of nature around me. So, it's up onto the line at the first opportunity, though of course, the track has long since been removed. Then, we pause for a few shots of the road ahead and our own shadow, which we are far too wise to chase. We head back in the direction of the car with the Rowan and the Scots Pine providing our honour guard above ripening blackberries that foretell better-than-average September foraging. Once again, I grow excited and marvel at the privilege of living in God's own country, the New Forest, where to my reckoning, you could walk every day of your life and never repeat your route precisely.

Then, quite suddenly, as we steer a straight path on a straight railway, the Shadow Man is walking beside us. The three of us proceed in silence for some time. I dare neither to speak nor to look directly at him for fear he will disappear once again. But somehow, at the same time, I feel a sense of reassurance knowing he has returned for a reason. Once, we were old sparring partners, the Shadow Man and I, circling each other cautiously, always keeping our sword hands free. But that time has long since passed. As I grew familiar with him all those years ago, I named him Cogitatis, for he made me think as no other ever did. But that, of course, was before I learned his real name. If you want to know more of him, take a look at *Forest Rain*, which is dedicated to him.

So, in the continuing silence, I focus once more on my work. My springtime work, my summer work and my coming autumn work. And I know now, there will be work right up to and throughout the winter. There is such relief in that knowledge, such congruence in the work. I am at my happiest by far, when I am addressing my appointed tasks in fulfilment of my contract.

We pass the spot where we should turn off the line for the car park, but walk on. Ahead is a low bridge. It carries the road over the railway line and in so doing, serves to provide shade to the ponies. They stand in the shadows, seeking respite from the sun that does not seem so hot to me. As we approach, they move a little uneasily in our presence and I see that they are a mother with a young foal. I have missed the new foals this year, so cumbered about have I been with matters of hearing. We stop, so as not to scare them and turn to reverse our steps back towards the car.

"You're back," I finally pluck up the courage to say to him. The Shadow Man smiles, looking towards the ground, his hands in his pockets. There is no sword at his side. It is years since we were combatants. Now, old brothers in arms, we have beaten those swords into ploughshares and know the joy of co-workmanship.

"Does this mean that we're going to be writing together again?" I ask.

He smiles. "And you thought this was about the seasons of the year," he answers.

7 Battle Scars

Where are your wounds? I see no blood upon you.

> You see no blood? It is because each day, I soak it up in
> smiles,
> masquerading happiness to all who come too close.

Where are your wounds? I hear you utter not a single cry of pain.

> You hear no cries?
> It is because I long since learned to weep in silence
> and only to my closest confidant, the wind.

Where are your wounds? I see no dust of battle clinging to you.

> You see no dust?
> It is because you will not look me in the eye,
> to see the listlessness of one who was interred,
> still breathing, under burial mounds of indifference.

Where are your wounds? Your clothing is not torn.

> You see no lacerations in these brightly coloured garments?
> There are none.

For they are burial sheets, wound tight to hold the living
dead.

Where are your wounds? You do not carry any stench of death.

You smell no death upon me,
for I have waded where the waters run soul-deep,
baptising me with determination.

Where are your wounds? I see no setting sun fall low upon a field
of battle.

You see no battlefield? No blood?
You hear no cries of pain?
This war was fought half a century ago.
The invader drove his armoured columns deep into my
sovereign lands,
annexed sanctuary cities,
laid landmines on the road to refuge.
I waved white flags,
but he refused to see them.
I called for peace but my voice was too small for him to
hear.
A refugee, I sought to flee in terror,
but he overwhelmed me,
day upon relentless day.

I trusted you.
I am your son and I was only five.

8. This is for the Hopeless Losers

This is for the hopeless losers
And the lonely & the weak
And the lost & the degraded
And the too dumb to speak

When The Day Goes Down
Annie Lennox & Dave Allan
Stewart

My hearing dog, Matt, retired last week. Twelve years as an active working dog has come to an end. Julie came down from Hearing Dogs for Deaf People and decommissioned him. Not that Matt knew, of course. He just goes on doing what he always did. But there is one crucial difference – he no longer has a legal right of access to places like shops and restaurants. And that has got me to thinking.

A couple of weeks before he retired, we did some shopping in Waitrose. We don't often go there any more. They are unashamedly more expensive than other supermarkets. But we were passing and the quality of what they sell is undeniable, so I made an exception. Now, let me assure you this is not going to turn into a rant against Waitrose for the way I get treated in there as a recipient of a hearing dog. I have been to many Waitrose stores over many years and never once have the folk that work there been anything less than wonderfully courteous, often taking a special interest in us, and at the very least beaming welcoming smiles at us. They really are fantastically well trained and their attitude is exemplary.

Sadly, that's not quite so true of the customers. This is only the second time a Waitrose customer has been rude to me on account of my disability, so I cannot generalise. But do I detect some sense of *'better-than-thou-because-I-can-afford-to-shop-here'*? Some *'you get a nicer class of person shopping in Waitrose and we don't want it tainted by the likes of you'*?

She came at me from behind and so caught me unawares. I have enough hearing to tell, sometimes, when someone is talking to me from behind; especially if it is in a loud voice; especially if the tone is aggressive. I turned to see who was addressing me. Her angry eyes peered at me derisively down a raised nose. It was obvious, even without hearing the words she spoke, that in this woman's opinion I was unfit to be scraped off the sole of her perfect green wellie. "Why have you brought your dog in here?" I lip read her disdainful demand. "This is a food shop. You shouldn't be in here."

Shouldn't be in here because I have a dog, I wondered, or because I'm disabled, or because you think you're better than me? Or was it all of the above? My response was instinctive and my instinct is to avoid confrontation – except when it involves disability. If I am berated on account of my disability, I tend to take it upon myself to act on behalf of the disabled community. "Read the coat," I answered in a controlled, neutral tone, motioning down to Matt in his uniform, "and you'll be able to answer your own question."

She squinted down at him, a hint of a snarl curling round the corners of her faultlessly applied lipstick. "He's a hearing dog," I continued, "and we have every legal right to be in this store. He even has clearance from the Chartered Institute of Health Inspectors. Do you want to see his credentials?"

I was already reaching into my pocket for Matt's ID, when she responded with her nose still high in the air and her eyes half closed in an attempt to preserve her sense of superiority in the face of her own crumbling confidence. "If you'll just listen..." I lip read.

"I can't," I responded. "I'm deaf. That's why I have the dog." As I turned to the relevant page in the ID book she stormed off muttering. Clearly, I was not the nicer class of shopper she was used to exchanging self-satisfied egotistical platitudes within Waitrose. I withdrew to lick my metaphorical wounds. I hurt myself when I am ungentle.

"For we are all the same," wrote Annie Lennox, "Underneath the shadows of the sun," in echo of the Apostle Paul who wrote, "For I say to every man that is among you, not to think of himself more highly than he ought to think."

Since Matt's retirement I have not been back to Waitrose. I have not felt like it quite honestly, particularly as I cannot be confident he would be granted entry, no longer having the legal entitlement (registered hearing dogs wear a distinctive maroon jacket and we have now exchanged his for one that reads 'Retired Hearing Dog'). But I did have another appointment this week to which I decided to take him. I have been scheduled for a cochlear implant later this year and two of the hoops to be jumped through are MRI and CT scans at University Hospital Southampton. It was perhaps not surprising that I attended with a degree of trepidation as to how we would be received, now that we didn't have the law on our side. As we stepped through the door of the MRI unit, behind the reception desk sat another lady of similar age to the one who had confronted us in Waitrose. She took one look at Matt and stood up. Then, she walked round the desk and said, "Oh, my goodness, he's wonderful! Can I talk to him?" I smiled in relief and said, "Of course," whereupon she dropped to one knee and proceeded to fuss and cuddle my retired hearing dog. Out from the scan room came a young man in hospital uniform. 'Trouble?' I wondered; but only until he too dropped to one knee and joined in the fuss-making. Matt was having a marvellous time! The only difficulty they had was in negotiating who would look after him while I had my scan.

Afterwards, we were led down to the CT scan room where quite spontaneously, exactly the same thing happened. Afterwards, I thanked everyone profusely for making the whole experience so pleasant and asked where I could get a coffee. The Marks & Spencer coffee shop by the entrance was recommended. So, I headed for M&S holding my breath – after all, you get a Waitrose class of shopper in M&S. I need not have worried. The same exemplary staff behaviour was in evidence. And when I asked to share a table in a rather full seating area, the assembled multitude came close to arguing over who would win the privilege of having the dog sit next to them. Matt got cuddled and fussed into a soporific trance and I was kept so busy answering everyone's questions I barely made it through coffee and a sandwich. Any moans about a dog on food premises? Or in the hyper-hygienic environment of a hospital? You bet your sweet life there weren't. You get a nicer class of customer in the University Hospital Southampton. And a very nice class of staff as well. In fact, there are a whole lot of very nice human beings in evidence there. Maybe, I should start buying my veg there, too.

9. Lucky Beggar

I reckon it was Geoff's fault at first. Until that visit to Prague, I had managed to pack The Pretender tightly away in the dusty back cupboard of my mind, labelled 'easier ignored'. I only look there on the very rare occasions when I'm spoiling for an argument or seeking some long forgotten value like honour – and only then, when the moral power's cut out and my value system grinds to a halt.

Each day, we strolled the cobbled streets and alleyways that bisected the tall, foreboding buildings, weaving a thread of conversation between the tourists and the traffic. From time to time, Geoff would break off in the middle of some deep debate about consumerism, or redemption or astral travel, and dig at the roots of his pocket and his conscience. You see, he had noticed The Charlatan, who would be kneeling in disguise, nose almost to the pavement, preferring the cold, hard ground to an honest day's work with his hands. And with words of warmth lost to my ears upon the biting winter wind, Geoff would press a coin or a note into the man's cupped palms.

And in between the heartbeats, where time is speechless,

I would wonder.

The next day, we would see The Charlatan once again, disguised this time as a one-legged alcoholic, pleading with his eyes for the misplaced philanthropy of the gullible, and Geoff would do the same thing all over again. Oblivious to the adroitness of my astute discourse, he would plunge his hands deep to retrieve a little piece of salvation (his own, you understand, not The Charlatan's), squat down on his haunches and in German, or French, or tongues of silence, pass a piece of hope to the fraud.

And as unease rippled in widening

circles across the plate-glass lake of my composure,

I would reassure myself with the very reliable left-brain logic,

that it is better to give to homeless charities

than to those that beg upon the streets.

When I saw The Charlatan next, he had disguised himself as a paraplegic outside the entrance to Santiago Cathedral. I was alone, delivering all my learned monologues internally to no one in particular. And since Geoff wasn't there to be ripped off, my left brain had only the right to argue with. You know, of course, that it never wins in such circumstances – myopic logic was never designed to withstand realities revealed to the emotional eye.

So, inside the cathedral, I reached into my pocket, just to see how it felt. I was conducting no more than a laboratory experiment, you understand.

I came out through the cathedral door and The Charlatan was waiting for me.

He raised his eyes to meet mine.

Our smiles embraced.

I touched his hand to give him a note.

And he gave me, God.

10. Transcending

I lived in fear
that you would one day see
the dark hard kernel of ego
that lay beneath the gentleness
I prefer to show you;

until I stood at the birthing of eternity,
watching the stars wake one by one,
when light deluged the Cosmos.

And then, I ceased to worry?
No.
I simply ceased.

11. All on My Own (don't wanna be)

Willing to experience aloneness
I discover connection everywhere

Jennifer Welwood
Unconditional

I walk to the top of the hill on winding, cobbled streets, barely wider in some places than the span of my arms. For perhaps, twenty minutes, I climb through the pre-dawn dark, pausing occasionally for breath, listening to the silence that is punctuated persistently by the cockerels as they interject their announcement of the coming day.

Set out below me are the white, flat-roofed buildings of the town, yet to come clearly into view with the morning light. Rows of streetlights stretch out into the distance and over the hill, lurching round the erratic bends in the road like columns of drunken soldiers. The sky is sharpened by lightning flashes of a storm somewhere out to sea. Fishing boats are beginning to emerge from the harbour some two or three miles distant, where they have lain protected from the night storms by the sea wall. There is no thunder. The storm will not pass this way. Now, the red sun rubs his eyes and rises through the mist that he will shortly burn away, as he gradually becomes more assertive in bestowing the day on Skyros. Commerce begins to break out below me and the sounds of activity impose themselves on my silence.

How did I come to be here? Let me tell you.

Week One
Day One

I have always disliked coach travel. Oh, it's not so bad on a long straight motorway, where you hurtle at seventy miles an hour or more, eating up the miles and drinking down the scenery, until you get to some urban bus station that looks precisely like the one you left. But as I write this, I am bouncing up and down on the back seat of one of those buses whose windows do not open. A cylindrical jet of pressurised air lunges down at me from the ceiling, and I am starting to feel nauseous. This is what I get for writing at the back of a bus. Still, as I have long since learned, I either write it at the moment of awareness or I do so not at all.

We had arrived in Athens on the previous evening after a hitch-free flight from Heathrow. However, I was less than delighted to learn this morning that we have a seven-hour transfer to the island of Skyros, which is our destination. At this stage of the journey, the party consists of between sixty and seventy people of varying ages and inclinations. We are united by a dislike of solitude, which evidenced itself last night at the bar, where we were all just a tad over-eager to make friends with the perfect strangers that will become our intimate associates for the next two weeks. I learn that when we arrive at Skyros we will be split into two groups – those based at the more bohemian beach holiday at Atsitsa, with its water sports and its bamboo huts, and the rest of the party heading for the Skyros Centre, where the accommodation is a little more courteous to the comfort zones and where the activity programme revolves more overtly around creativity and spiritual growth. No prizes for guessing which centre I'm heading for. I am here to explore writing as a healing activity. And besides, I never really did learn to balance on my windsurf board for long enough to change tack.

I am delighted that I have already had one conversation of worth on the flight over with Nancy, the young woman in the seat next to me on the aircraft, and it seems to me more than coincidence that she, too, is here not only to enjoy a holiday but also to explore consequential issues at a watershed in her life. I will discover later that, of the thirty-five or so people heading for the Skyros Centre, most are at a turning point in their lives or are seeking new directions. A generation or two ago, we might have been churchgoers heading out on a pilgrimage to the Holy Land, but the world keeps turning, and the methodologies of exploring the human condition turn with it.

After seven hours of getting on and off coaches that bounce us about the winding hill roads, and ferries that throw us up and down in sea storms, we dock at the port on Skyros. Mercifully, the final leg of our journey is a mere twenty-minute coach transfer to the town of Skyros itself.

There have been numerous points at which the journey could have gone disastrously wrong for me. I booked my taxi to Heathrow two hours later than I should have done (courtesy of my head being perpetually in the clouds) and I omitted to attend to the small matter of getting off the bus when we arrived in the town of Skyros (courtesy of being deaf and unable to hear tannoys), to name but two. But there is an unfamiliar calm that has descended upon my normally tumultuous soul that inspires me with a confidence that my presence here is purposeful. I am convinced that there is a consequential work that I am here to do.

Day Two

Thirty-five of us seep into the dining area at the Skyros Centre, to get the usual acclimatisation talk that comes as part of most holiday packages, together with the rather less usual explanations of what the activity programme here will amount to for the next two weeks. For the first week's activity, I select Yoga, Writing as Healing and Greek Cookery. I'm confident about the writing – the most important programme to me. We all find security in that which comes naturally to us and we all have a tendency to sit within the comfort zone. Skyros is going to offer me a safe enough environment to stretch some of those comfort zones, but not just yet. What I have not given much thought to is the process of getting to know people and the consequences of not doing so. I have to admit that as the first week presses on, it turns out not to be the programmes themselves that are central to my learning.

As the days unfold, I become increasingly reminded that group interaction is difficult for me, largely because of the difficulty of hearing a multiplicity of voices in quick succession. So, it happens as it usually happens. I start by trying to participate in a conversation, fail to hear what it is about and then, without realising it, slip away into trance. I return a while later, having not the slightest idea of what is being discussed around me, conscious only of the sense of exclusion that auditory isolation brings. As the pattern repeats itself at dinner, in bars, in groups as we walk down the street, I start to read more into the pattern than is valid and experience the sense of rejection that we all fear so much. Because of the human tendency to focus selectively, it seems to me that I am being excluded, that no one wants to talk to me. I then start to feel sorry for myself. I think only of the periods of silence when I am not engaging with other people and I forget the meaningful discussions that I have experienced. I fail to register the fact that, from time to time, just about everyone finds themselves standing on the touchline rather than playing the game.

The shirt-sleeves learning kicks in on the second day. A group walk is arranged to a high point in the town where there is an excellent view and a stature of Rupert Brooke (buried on the island in 1915 following his death at sea). By dint of being late out of the WC, I miss the party's departure and head off in an attempt to catch up with them. The random turns to purposeful, when I take a wrong turning and end up at a quiet little square with a tiny Greek Orthodox chapel, that looks down over a stunning view across the coastline. I stop while the wind wafts a gentle breeze through my hair, conscious of my solitude. As the silence permeates, I permit my consciousness to settle on the aloneness I normally do so much to avoid. Gradually, I become aware that I am afraid of 'alone'. But for once, I start to think about it instead of avoiding it. Why is 'alone' frightening? Why is it bad? And then, the awareness starts to come and I begin to realise why I have taken that wrong turn that has enabled me to sit in solitude overlooking the bay. 'Alone' is only bad because I habitually reach outside myself for validation, for reassurance that I have worth. For co-dependence is the process of seeking a sense of validation of self-worth outside yourself. If you run this pattern, it follows that when you are alone, confirmation of your worth is absent.

The thoughts are slotting into place like jigsaw pieces now, and I am excited and frightened all at the same time. I do not want to explore this issue because it is dangerous. But at the same time, I do want to explore it because it contains understanding and perhaps solutions to why I am prone to feeling so bad about me.

I look the demon full in the eyes now, for perhaps the first time ever, and I find he is made of ice. I discover that if I confront the source of my fear, it begins to melt around the edges. I have lived under an unconscious presupposition that I only have worth to the extent that the feedback from others confirms me to have worth. It is hardly surprising that the absence of such feedback is frightening. Rejection, being unloved, is the most terrifying state known to beast or to man or to spirit. But if you start, instead, from the presumption that you *are* worthy, everything changes. Each moment alone is not to be read as rejection that confirms your unacceptability. It is no more than what it is – a moment alone. It carries no subtle messages, no deeper meaning. In so realising, you can *stop* reading meaning into it. And if you read no meaning into it, it is not to be feared. You can also stop carrying the baggage of presumed worthlessness around with you when you meet other people.

And then, I finally see it: it was always that presumption – that I am of no worth, that I have no value – that betrayed itself in my demeanour and my conversation, that I used unconsciously to push people away, to repulse the very validation I so craved. For in the topsy-turvy world of co-dependence and low self-esteem, I cannot process feedback that tells me that I have value, for it contradicts the sense of self that I have embraced. The circle is so vicious, it might as well have venom-filled fangs.

As if this revelation is not enough on its own, I then realise – and here comes the biggie – that if these things are true for me, they are likely to be true for others as well. Can it actually be the case that pretty much everyone else out there is doing the same thing to a greater or lesser degree? Virtually all of us seek external confirmation of our worth. It is at this point that I realise that in addressing co-dependence, it is the very epicentre of the human condition that I have stumbled upon. My journey to the centre of the earth is over. I have found the source of turmoil in my soul. Gradually, the realisation grows that I am blessed beyond measure. Finally, to have been led to this point; that my spirit guides indeed are there, and that their own periodic silences, far from indicating absence or disinterest, have been purposeful in gently guiding me to this place. No, my journey is not over, for there is substantial work still to be done on the issues and many further Learnings still to be revealed. But here, at last, is the centre of the darkness in my soul and that of potentially every other man or woman that walks the face of the planet.

After perhaps an hour of sitting up there in the stillness of that little piazza, looking out over the windy sea while the words of life blow about my spirit, I know it is time to descend into the lowlands again. As I make my way back down, I ask my spirit guides to help me work through and deal with this issue. To my amazement, for the first in my life, they decline to help. They say that it is intrinsic to dealing with this particular matter that I find the solution inside and not outside – not even as far outside as with them. And then, the reason becomes obvious. For I realise that my reaching out to them at that moment is yet another example of how I seek external validation. I am naive enough to ask also how long it will take, but again, they are silent. Then, I weigh and value that silence, acknowledging that it will take a week, or a year, or a lifetime to pass through this Learning. I must cross this territory alone, for aloneness is part of the solution.

I also acknowledge, now, that when I arrive at closure on the principle of the issue, the work of addressing its effects will continue. For I realise that I run habit patterns based on my deep-rooted fears. Even when I have rolled the stone away from the grave and let in the sunshine that will melt the ice-demon, the wastewater of habit will still take time to soak away. I am reminded of the words of the Tao Te Ching that talk of 'unlearning'. There will be much unlearning in changing the habit patterns of co-dependence. However, the possibility of changing patterns only really opens to us when we draw them into the light of consciousness and ask ourselves whether they are a help or a hindrance to us.

Days Three to Six

So, now that I start to reposition solitude in my thinking, I begin to see that time alone is valuable time. Perhaps by coincidence and perhaps by purpose, I now also begin to relax more around others; begin to accept that my physiological condition means that both I and others around me need to make more than the average level of effort to communicate; begin to realise that if I do not get the gist of the conversation or the punchline of a joke, it does not mean I am a social outcast. It meant no more and no less than I did not hear; that I can be included as much or as little as anyone else, as much or as little as I choose.

By the midpoint of the holiday, I am beginning to imbibe the Learnings of co-dependence for which I have come to Skyros. I had come to deal with the issues raised by a perpetual search for validation outside myself that most, if not all of us make until we learn better, more integrated ways of being. I have begun to see that I reach unconsciously for validation; that I read the behaviour of others as confirming my worth by acknowledging me, or as denying my worth by failing to acknowledge me.

I am reminded, also, that people believe and behave as they do because of what is inside them, because of the map of the world that they employ, not because of the map I employ. They live by their own maps, dealing with our common reality from their own perspectives. I cannot impute my meaning into their behaviour. And thus, I affirm my intention to listen consciously to the inward voice of intuition that is commonly quieter than the self-talk of doubt and self-deprecation. I am deciding I will consciously seek my validation on the inside, not the outside.

The awareness I am gaining comes not so much from the writing group in which I participate, as in the countless informal interactions I pursue, together with the silences that I pass through and that pass through me. I have understood that all of us have the same hunger in our hearts. If we draw near enough to another person to enable them to feel safe enough to lift their veneer a little, we discover it to be the same for them as it is for us. It begins to feel safe to open up to another person, if we have learned to refer for our validation to the soul within, not to the environment without. When I know it is enough to be as I am, then I know it is safe to reveal that 'me' to others. Any criticism or negativity that I might engender in so doing, is about what is in them, not what is in me. The conclusion from this? That it is time to open up, to send love, light and peace, to let go of the sorrows of personal histories and the yearnings for personal futures of completing myself – it is enough to be who I am in this moment and to be so independent of any other individual.

Day Seven

I have seen it now, this creature of the shadows that lurked just outside the illumination of the firelight. He was wont to step into the light only when the embers of human interaction burned low and the darkness ruled in silence. I have seen his binding, incarcerating energy that constitutes the emotional self-abuse of co-dependence. In a little Greek Orthodox chapel by the sea, a mile out of Atsitsa, I light a candle and send energy to a dear friend who believes at that moment that she may have cancer. I settle in the half-light on a stone bench before the icons that represent the spiritual awareness of other men and women and ease into trance to channel to her some of the energy she needs.

And there, intending to feed energy outwards in the economy

spirit, I find I am fed simultaneously with energy and awareness flowing inwards. I see my old pattern of grasping at the souls of others for fear of losing their esteem. I see that I used that esteem to bolster my identity at a time when it was beyond my comprehension that anyone should choose to hold me for nothing more than love – no obligation, no ties, simply the care for someone they value.

I become aware, now, that it is only by the creation of new habitual patterns, the confronting of fear, the taking of risk and the understanding that others react to what is in them, not what is in me, that I will root another perception of self-worth, sending tendrils down into the rich humus of my underlying identity. And when the work is done and I stand sufficient in myself, when I no longer come to others for bolstering and shoring up, then it is that I will be able to step into a relationship of mutual edification and up-building, for I shall reach within and know my value and my sufficiency. Then, I shall cast off the discarded snakeskin of co-dependence, emerging into a deeper awareness of my worth.

Day Twelve

I walk to the top of Skyros town, up through the winding, uneven stone streets, barely wider in some places than the span of my arms. For perhaps twenty minutes, I climb through the pre-dawn dark, pausing occasionally for breath, listening to the silence that is punctuated persistently by the cockerels, as they interject their announcement of the coming day.

At the very top of the town, I am back in the plaza where I started on that second day, where the little chapel keeps sentry duty through the night. I sink gratefully onto the bench to cool off from my climb.

Set out below me, are the white flat-roofed buildings of the town, yet to come clearly into view with the morning light. Rows of streetlights stretch out into the distance and over the hill, lurching round the erratic bends in the road like columns of drunken soldiers. The sky is sharpened by distant lightning flashes of a storm somewhere out at sea. The boats are beginning to emerge from the harbour, some two or three miles distant, where they have lain protected from the night storms by the sea wall. There is no thunder. The storm will not pass this way. Now, the red sun rubs his eyes and rises through the mist that he will shortly burn away, as he gradually becomes more assertive in bestowing the day on Skyros. Commerce begins to break out below me and the sounds of activity impose themselves on my silence.

As the light comes up, I take out my pen to write. This Learning is not done. It may yet take this lifetime to complete.

12. Passive Lover

I have fallen in love with a mannequin.
I dress her in Dior and Channel,
buy her Gucci and Jimmy Choos.

At weekends, we drive to the coast in my XK convertible,
her long blonde hair rippling out behind her in the wind.
Come evening, we sit before a hardwood fire where
I toss pine cones into the flames and
pour Chateau d'Yquem into lead crystal goblets.

As the glowing embers cool, I carry her gently to a four-poster
bed
where I whisper words of love into her ear.

In the morning, I wake alone.
What more could I have done to keep her?

13. Strictly No Dancing

Setting myself up for failure

"I want to dance, and you don't dance."

It was one of the many reasons my ex-wife had given for not returning home after she had left me. Most of them were rather more profound than this one, but for some reason the phrase had stayed particularly, prominently in my mind throughout the disconnection process.

Though the absence of dance in my life never left me with a particular sense of loss, it had always been a matter of some interest to me as to why I did not dance. Ironically, on the few occasions on which I had been enticed onto a dance floor, usually after the application of fairly copious quantities of alcohol, I had been told that I was actually quite good at it. Naturally, I filtered such information out, for we are prone to dismissing feedback that does not fit our image of ourselves, quietly emptying into the waste bin of incredulity much that could be useful and energising to us. Generally, though, I was too self-conscious and carried too negative a body image to risk stepping onto a dance floor. This emanated from both low self-esteem generally, and, I believe, a specific incident that occurred in my childhood.

I remember – and I guess, I must have been about five at the time – my parents took my brother and me to a social event being staged for cub scouts' families. Peter, being older than me, was a cub, and being a cub was groovy. Of course, pretty much anything Peter did that I, by dint of age or size, was unable to do was groovy by definition. Of course, another forty years or so has changed 'groovy' to 'cool', but you get the idea. I was too young to be a cub and anyway, I was not groovy. But we all attended the social in the scouts' hut where there were eats and drinks and music and dancing. During an interval when no one was dancing but the music was still playing, I took it upon myself to get up and do the Twist (well it was the 1960s!), whereupon some woman who was sitting a few places away and evidently found my choreographic interpretations endearing, pointed me out to her husband, who also looked at me and smiled. Well, cognitive dissonance reared its head above the waves and I felt suddenly self-conscious, presuming myself to be being criticised. Quickly, I sat down, chastened, and withdrew into my shell.

However, the real burn came later in the evening when without any warning at all, my father suddenly grabbed me, lifted me to his chest and swung me round and round the dance floor to the immense amusement, or so it seemed to me, of the assembled multitude. The sense of powerlessness and ridicule was crushing beyond my ability to express it even now. Everything in me wanted to get away from him and that place and those people at that moment. I kicked his thighs as violently as I could with my short little legs and tried to beat him with fists that he had pinned to my sides. I roared and screamed at him to stop as he continued to swing me round in a grotesque parody of ballroom competition dancing. Of course, he didn't see it that way. For him it was simply a bit of fun, an opportunity to attract some humour and draw some energy as a result. He never knew what it was for me to be on the receiving end of that experience.

I have long since made my peace with my father and my

memories of him. But that particular memory, discharged as it now is of its emotional sting, reminds me of the damage it is possible for the powerful to inflict upon the powerless. It long remained one of the underlying experiences that left me disinclined to yield control and to resist stepping out onto a dance floor. As I was to find out, dance consistently stands as a metaphor for numerous patterns that we run more widely in our lives, often connected with leadership and power.

There is no reward without risk

So, what was it that changed, such that I could find myself in a tango class on Skyros? And indeed, what business did a self-respecting tango class have flirting with a rather weird holistic vacation in Greece anyway?

Well, as to the first question – what changed? – I guess the only answer is that it was I who had changed. And the catalyst for that change at that moment was the Skyros experience itself. There is something about bringing together thirty or so spiritually hungry and self-aware people who feel the need for re-evaluation and change and engendering in them a sense of permissive safety in which to explore themselves and their interactions with one another. Within a week, most of us were opening up to one another and to the many learnings available to those who chose to draw on them.

It was at the end of the first week that a social event was arranged which included, amongst other things, an opportunity to receive some structured dance tuition. It is not something I would intuitively have undertaken given my propensities, but that evening, I had been chatting in the bar to an American woman in her sixties who had done a million interesting things with her life. When the dance event commenced, she told me that she would like to participate. Some combination of Skyros safety, a reasonable quantity of Malibu and orange, and the enjoyment of the lady's company enticed me onto the dance floor, where John Harris proceeded to offer seductively easy tuition in a Latin American dance known as the Merengue. As we proceeded through each movement in the dance, the process was instantly enjoyable. I was on a dance floor and – good grief – I was having fun. Something had shifted in my habitual inward focus, my negative body image and my fear of dance. My guard was down and I could permit myself to take pleasure in the movements of my own body and my rapport with a dance partner. An opportunity had slipped in under my defences to deal with at least one of my limiting beliefs – that bodily, I'm a poor quality specimen and any physical activity I undertake will lead to grief.

Well, the issue did not end there. I had intended to spend the main tuition time of my second week on Skyros in a writing class on "writing as healing", tutored by a spiritually aware and talented writer by the name of Allegra Taylor. But my experience on the dance floor that evening enticed me to stretch the elastic of my comfort zone to the point of transparency and take John Harris's class, "Tango - more than a dance".

Week Two
Day 1: Adonis and Venus

Now, my vast experience of dance classes (just kidding!) is that they are populated by two kinds of people. There are those whose bodies bear a fair resemblance to Adonis or Venus and whose minds are so attuned that they can absorb the expertise of the teacher instantly by osmosis. Then, there is the occasional individual, always male, usually in his late forties, present because his mother has told him it is "time to find a nice young lady". He peers out at you through bifocals under hair that is no longer on speaking terms with the shampoo bottle, whilst sporting a shirt that betrays a more intimate familiarity with the ketchup bottle. Mercifully, we were not such a class. Well, the odd Venus or two was present (Adonis had a prior with his manicurist) but they seemed content to slum it with those of us who leaned instinctively more to the ketchup bottle.

John structured his class as two periods of about an hour each, split by a coffee break. An hour of posture and step was followed by an hour of leading and following or, as he termed it, 'inviting' and 'listening'. Now, that kind of reframe was guaranteed to draw my attention to the life-learnings yet to come. My first hour contained no other surprises except one. Within a few minutes of John's opening remarks on correct posture, two of our number withdrew for reasons of particular physical issues they found incompatible with the posture and movement required by Tango. I pondered on the fact that had it been me that felt a need to withdraw (as I was to do later in the week), I would have struggled with embarrassment, a sense of failure and an uneasily feeling of abandoning the group. Evidently, not everyone feels it is unacceptable to concentrate on their own needs at times.

But it was in the second session of the first day that the learning began to pique my curiosity, as I started to understand the way that dance can draw our underlying patterns into the light of physical expression, where we can imbibe the learning consciously – if we have the eyes to see, that is.

It was hardly surprising that that first experience of 'inviting and listening' began to raise immediate – if unconscious – issues for many of us, to do with our habitual patterns of leadership and followership, control and power. I was first paired with a young woman by the name of Dee. We were instructed to undertake the role of leader and follower in an exercise that required us each to place hands upon the other's arms, sway together until we had entered into a common sense of rhythm, then move around the floor following no particular steps. We decided (or perhaps it was just Dee that decided) that Dee would lead first and off we went. As we progressed around the dance floor, I became quickly aware of how easily I slipped into the role of being led. So much was this the case, that a whole set of issues began bubbling up into my consciousness concerning whether I find myself too easily led in life, generally. The old sea serpent of co-dependence had begun to raise its scaly head about the waves of self-awareness once again.

When the time came to switch around and I took the lead, I found myself in a more challenging role. For though in a business context, leadership generally comes to me fairly easily, the same comfort never attaches itself to me in social situations. Added to a general sense of uncertainty was the fact that I was new to this, and not confident in what I was doing. Consequently, my leadership of my partner around the floor was uncertain. When we are ambiguous in leadership, we cannot expect those who are meant to follow to do so easily or gracefully, for we engender no confidence and communicate no clear instruction.

Now Dee, being the self-confident type, began to get a tad impatient at my meagre efforts, and was clearly of the opinion that she knew better than I did how I ought to be leading her. Thus, I found myself undergoing the interesting experience of being led in my leadership by my follower. It wasn't that she said anything, but rather that she resisted my indications that we ought to move in a given direction and tried to demonstrate by resistance and tension in her own body, the direction in which she thought we should be moving. Not surprisingly, we found ourselves gripping onto each other and looking into each other's eyes in quivering indecision, rooted to the spot, not sure of who was doing what, our joint motion resembling fairly closely the panicked convulsions of a couple of gasping fishes thrown up onto a beach.

John had mercy upon us and drew the session to a close with a debrief. It became evident that I was not the only one processing issues and seeing metaphors, for Dee later admitted, a little self-consciously, that she had enjoyed leading rather too much for her own comfort and found herself going control crazy out there on the floor. The dance class was proving to be educational for a number of us on more levels than one.

Day Two: Awareness is the beginning of change

I have found in group situations in the past, that my confidence tends to ebb and flow with the gaining and implementation of new knowledge. Flushed with the possession of some slight expertise that I did not previously possess, I can delude myself into thinking, momentarily, that I am an expert, elegant in my execution of my new skill. Then, I make a mistake, feel embarrassment again, and I'm back in the scout hut having been spied doing the Twist, wanting the floor to open its jaws and swallow me whole.

However, something else happened at the beginning of day two. I was so busy focussing my attention inside, processing all the new learning at the level of personal development, that I did not hear the next instruction that John issued. I was jolted unceremoniously back into the room when the music started again and I watched everyone else proceeding confidently around the dance floor while I had not a clue what to do. The learning here was clear – you can't be inside processing and outside paying attention to what you should be doing at one and the same time.

It is rather important to choose your moment for doing each appropriately! Indeed, as a result of not having absorbed that particular lesson appropriately, I went to the side of the room and sat out that round, slipping further and further into confusion and self-conscious embarrassment based on forgotten experiences from who knows how many years or how many lifetimes ago. In fact, I lost all power to process until John came along and asked me what was wrong. Interestingly, that one intervention was enough to break the pattern and draw my attention outward again, enabling me to function normally once more. Yet another aspect of co-dependence was coming into the light of consciousness for me to judge, and accept or reject as I considered fit.

Awareness of our patterns is the beginning of the opportunity to change them if we wish to do so. I needed to remind myself once again that a momentary inability to function does not diminish me at the identity level. My embarrassment was immaterial, since everyone else was concentrating on their own issues anyway.

I am reminded of the statement in Don Miguel Ruiz's book, *The Four Agreements*: "Nothing others do is because of you. What others say and do is a projection of their own reality, their own dream. When you are immune to the opinions and actions of others, you won't be the victim of needless suffering."

Day Three: It's not my fault, so it must be yours

As the class commenced, I eased back into the swing of it and found myself partnered with Kathy, a rather less confident woman than Dee. As we again practised following and leading, Kathy would be confused if I did not lead through the set pattern of steps we had learned. With some interest, I noted that some of us, perhaps all of us, have trouble being led outside the scope of our expectations.

Dee, by contrast, was busy blaming her new partner for getting something else wrong. I found myself wondering how many of us seek to project failure of partnerships outwards onto our partner and thus deflect our own attention and that of others away from the contribution to the breakdown we have ourselves made. I rather think when a partnership falls apart, the issue is not so much what I did wrong, or what you did wrong, but rather that we both stopped putting the interests of the partnership first, focussing on what we ourselves want to do. To make a dance partnership work well for both parties, it is essential that each puts aside personal interests and concentrates on functioning with the other as a single unit.

Sometimes, when partnerships break down in the dance of life, we simply cannot allow ourselves to see our contribution to the breakdown for fear of the damage it would do us at the identity level if we acknowledged fault in ourselves. Many of us are apt to take the view that if I have done something wrong (activity) it means I'm not a nice person, or deficient, or unacceptable (identity). Commonly, we are too afraid to confront that particular demon. It is beyond sad that we cannot, for it prevents us realising how unwarranted the presumption is that poor quality actions imply an unacceptable identity. We focus on the failures of others, real or manufactured to deflect our attention from our own failures. In doing so, we prevent ourselves from confronting and understanding our own behaviour.

Our behaviour, all behaviour, is about patterns – responses to inward and outward stimuli. I know of no other way to change those patterns than to draw them into the light of consciousness, so that they can be examined and a choice be made as to whether they are still useful to us. Often, it is challenging for us to do that, for consciously or unconsciously, we fear a terrifying 'truth': that they mean we are bad people and therefore, unacceptable; and if unacceptable – worthless, invalid and that ultimately, that we must cease to exist.

So, we continue to run those patterns in unconscious response to stimuli that are more about what happened twenty years ago or twenty lifetimes ago than about present circumstances. Because we are too afraid to look at them, we do not get the opportunity to change them.

Surely, personal growth is ultimately about awareness. It is beyond sad that we deny ourselves the chance for change and development, for being at peace with ourselves, simply because we are afraid of looking at who we are and what we do. Such fear, it seems to me, is a fundamental element in the human condition. It is when we conquer it that we move forward and grow, that we proceed with the work that we came here to do.

John closed the class that day with two observations. Firstly, that leadership in dance needs to be stronger when we wish to elicit a change of direction in our partner. Having achieved the change, the grip of the inviter on the listener can be loosened somewhat and both partners can relax into the new motion until the time again comes for change. His second observation was that the strongest people are often the ones that have the most difficulty being led on the dance floor. The listener has to accept and respond to an instruction before the inviter can issue another instruction.

The connection between leadership on the dance floor and the way we use and respond to leadership and power in our lives was becoming impossible to ignore. I left the class deep in thought and went off to process the learnings that were now flowing freely. I concluded firstly that leadership is not about control, and followership is not about acquiescence. Rather, the two together are about rapport and elegance in cooperative activity that cannot be undertaken by one alone. Seen this way, the proper use of power (and all of us both exercise it and are subject to it in some degree) is emphatically not about dominance – the taking another's energy by force. On the contrary, it is a tool for the execution of tasks and the achievement of objectives.

I realised that leaders need to give instructions in such a way as to permit adequate time for followers to respond. Instruct too fast and the follower gets confused, the rapport breaks and the dance stops. I saw, too, that small instructions, properly communicated, elicit magnified responses – we do not need to over-instruct if we instruct congruently. A well-timed expert intervention can bring lasting beneficial change to ourselves or another. The satisfaction comes not from building your own ego as a wise teacher or a good instructor, but from knowing you have brought benefit to another. We are all, at different times, both leaders and followers, inviters and listeners, receivers of instructions and imparters of instructions, imparters of energy and growth and receivers of illumination from the light others carry – for that is the symbiosis of humanity.

Finally, I concluded, we will only be led if we want to be led. When we are too busy, off doing what we ourselves want to do, we cannot hear the instructions that come through our bodies. The inviter cannot successfully issue another instruction until the listener has acted upon the first.

I was beginning to see that this was not so much a dance class, as a lesson in how to live.

Day Four: there is no failure, only feedback

I was taken by surprise on the last day. John chose to start the class with some Yoga, since it has an application to dance. Given that I need to see people talk in order to hear them, I perhaps ought to have withdrawn from that particular part of the session. It is hard to see someone talking when you are flat on your back trying to stretch your left big toe around your right ear! Added to that, being more your Bacchus type than Adonis, I find Yoga difficult, and at the time of writing, that raises negative feelings for me. That will change as I grow, but for now, it is a reality I live with.

However, I am prone to acquiescing, and I attempted the Yoga and unwisely allowed a build-up of negative feelings to take place. As a result, I started the dance class proper in a state that was not well-tuned for enthusiastic learning. I had been slipping behind (in my estimation anyway) in the technical learning of Tango the previous day, and I had not integrated that learning properly. In short, I had failed to take account of my own capacity for learning and my own habitual speed of absorbing information. So, I stood in the class, slipping in and out of trance, missing more and more information and stuck in a state in which I could not process effectively. Gradually, I spiralled down and down, slipping into the old internal self-talk about my own worthlessness. And yes, it is still there when I look hard for it in the poorly lit back alleys and the rubbish skips of my mind. Now, my sense of obligation to others arising from co-dependent tendencies would normally have kept me in that class, experiencing suffering and feeling I was failing, out of some misplaced sense of loyalty. But this time, I did not do that. This time, my sense of self-worth had shifted sufficiently into the internal plane and I could see that the benefit of extracting myself from painful circumstances outweighed the fear of disapproval from staying. I broke state and got out of the situation I was finding dysfunctional.

I left the class and sat down at random in the lounge one floor down from the dance room to catch my breath physically and metaphorically. Still holding some of the negative feelings, I did not want talk to anyone. So, I picked up a guitar someone had left lying around and extemporised on it for a few moments – the neurology in my hands still retained the hand movements that made music, even if my ears could not hear it. It was then that by 'chance' I spied a pre-publication copy of *Forest Rain* that somebody had left on the lower shelf of the coffee table. I smiled, knowing that my guides were talking to me in the unpredictable juxtaposition of circumstance, reminding me that there was more to me than the negative patterns I sometimes exhibit, that I have value and that I had moved a long way forward from where I had been when those patterns were first formed. Then, a dear lady, Rachel, was kind enough to compliment me on the guitar playing, offering still more healing energy. So, I picked up *Forest Rain* and read the Learning titled *Reflections*, a piece about change and integration and leaving behind those aspects of our lives that we no longer need. Somewhat more energised, I slipped down into the town for a coffee and a croissant and a chance to finish the first draft of this Learning.

I did not complete the dance class that day, but I did imbibe the illumination I was there to receive. In that newly acquired light, I saw that we learn at a pace that is ecological for our own system and that our guides will only teach us at that pace. I saw that we always retain free will to remain where we are or to move somewhere more energising as we choose. I saw that that choice, though never dismissive of the interests of others, must ultimately be exercised in the context of our own needs. I was reminded, and learned again, that my worth does not depend on what I know, or write, or do, but rather subsists in the whole of who I am, in the astonishing perfection in which I was made, but still growing, ever growing.

I have chosen to dance again and have booked a Salsa class at home in the knowledge that if I can absorb the lessons of dance at a pace suitable for me, it is pleasurable and exciting. But should I choose not to proceed with dance, I will not beat myself up for it in former characteristic pattern. A long time ago, a dear friend repeatedly told me to be gentle with myself. I now have a clearer understanding of what that means. I shall deal with myself and the path I walk at a pace that is ecological to my system and elegant in my soul.

I have learned of leading and following, of introspection and external awareness, of the proper exercise of authority and power. I will continue to learn and explore in pain and in pleasure, continue to wonder with awe at the patterns that make up my unique identity, both the ones I wish to change and the ones that are helpful to retain.

The dance we dance is long, as long as it needs to be, for we wear no competitor numbers upon our backs and no judges score our performance. There are simply the tools and times we are offered over as many lifetimes as we need in order to grow from perfection to perfection – if we will but have eyes to see what we are doing.

I am content for this interlude of growth on Skyros to end now, for it has taught me more than I could ever have hoped about co-dependence about leadership and followership, about looking within and reaching without. It has reminded me of what I always knew and wrote in a poem that will never be put into the public domain:

> *God hath spake.*
> *Thou art a man.*
> *It is enough.*

Love, light and peace to you.

14. Time's Fool

20

When I first began to look for a man
I was seeking for someone to love me.
So I danced in the disco from LA to Frisco
just looking for someone to love me.
I was on the attack. I was great in the sack –
but I just wanted someone to love me.
Now I'm smothered in make-up and quick on the take-up
and pretty soon someone will love me.
My heels are six inch; getting guys is a cinch!
And someone out there's gonna love me.

30

Now I drink Gin and Tonic; my style is iconic.
I'm confident someone will love me.
My beauty's cosmetic, my boobs are synthetic
and all cos I want you to love me.
Hey, you look debonair. Let's have an affair!
Cos I really do want you to love me.
Your house is palatial – just pay for my facial –
I'm certain that soon you will love me.
You drive a Ferrari? Take me on safari
for honeymoon – that's where you'll love me!

40

We've got friends, ten a penny, but haven't got any
who'll help me to get you to love me.
I'll give birth to your baby, then maybe – just maybe –
there'll be someone here who will love me.
My beauty is heightened. I've had my teeth whitened
in order to get you to love me.
I've been under the knife just because I'm your wife.
So why is it you still won't love me?

50

You used to caress me – so why have you left me?
I just wanted to know that you loved me.
Now, I dress in Chanel and I wear it so well
cos I really want someone to love me.
I'm smothered in Lancôme, so why won't a man come
who'll take me away and just love me?

60

Now my age I'm defying – so why am I crying?
All I want is for someone to love me.

70

There's no one to love me. Love's too far above me.
Please, tell me why I cannot love me.

15. Plugging a Few Leaks

Back in the antediluvian past of the mid-1970s, I was studying political science at university. With the resignation of Richard Nixon in 1974, the whole issue of Watergate was central to the study of American politics, and I was asked to write a paper on the subject for one of my tutorials. It seems an awfully long time ago now, but one of the pieces of information I remember noting, was that the team Nixon used to try to stem the flow of unauthorised classified information from the White House into the public domain was known as 'The Plumbers'. Further enquiry as to why they were so named led to the discovery of one of those stories that is near impossible to prove once the tides of history have washed the salt of anecdote into the sands of fact. The tale goes that one of the members of Nixon's team was asked by a maiden aunt what he was doing for a living. He is reputed to have answered that he was plugging a few leaks at the White House. Thereafter, the lady concerned boasted proudly to her friends and neighbours that her nephew was a White House Plumber. Thus, the legend was born.

I have been having a few leaks of my own plugged this week. Well, to be more precise, I have had visits from two plumbers to deal with a blockage in the waste pipe from my kitchen. A couple of weeks ago, I noticed the cupboard under the kitchen sink was wet. Further investigation over several days led me to the conclusion that the waste pipe from the dishwasher was blowing water back as it emptied. Now, I like to think I am a man in control of my life and my environment. I decided that real men like me ought to be able to deal with a minor inconvenience such as this. So, I marched confidently down to my local plumbers' merchants and asked for a drain rod device and some suitable chemical cleaner. Evidently the word 'novice' was stamped in fluorescent dye on my forehead, since the guy behind the counter eyed me as if to say, "Are you *really sure* you ought to be doing this?" My disdainful unspoken answer was, "Yup, I'm great at DIY." He then proceeded to sell me the requisite items with a somewhat 'seen-it-all-before-and-it-will-come-to-grief' look on his face. Was I ever scornful! Yes, I should have known better. Numberless wonky shelves, smouldering electrical connections and leaky pipes for which I have been responsible over the years, bear eloquent testimony to the fact that DIY is not amongst my foremost callings in this lifetime.

Nevertheless, I'm pretty good at filtering out information I don't want to listen to, and I knew that if I called a plumber it would likely cost a fair bit, not to mention the damage it would do my pride. So, I ignored the warning signs and headed for home with my DIY problem-solving kit under my arm. Arriving home, I disconnected the waste pipe at a suitable point and slid the drain rod in. It went in to its whole length and didn't hit up against any blockage. Puzzled, I put the kettle on while I thought the matter through. I drank a cup of tea whilst still continuing to think about it. Surprisingly, neither the boiling of the kettle nor the drinking of the tea cleared the blockage.

I chastened myself for wasting £5.23 on a drain cleaning kit that had not solved the problem. Well, there was nothing for it but to use the chemical. The guy at the plumbers' merchants had assured me this was powerful stuff and would unquestionably solve my problem. I was not so reassured by the skull and crossbones logo on the box nor the warning 'Sulphuric Acid – use only as directed'. But then, I'm an expert DIY-er and we technical types know about these things. Warnings are for wimps. Tentatively, I poured the appropriate quantity of chemical into the sink waste (and yes, I had remembered to reconnect the waste pipe under the sink... what do you think I am, stoopid or summin'?). There was a hissing and gurgling, clear evidence that the compound was doing its job. So, as directed, I waited for five minutes, during which I read the newspaper and had another cup of tea. The next step in the process was to put the same quantity of water down the sink as I had already put chemical. There was a further satisfying gurgling, elevating my confidence in my DIY ability to hitherto unscaled heights. I waited the requisite further five minutes, during which I did what an Englishman does at these times (more tea), and then returned to the sink, flush with confidence that I could now flush my problem away.

I turned on the tap (that's a faucet if you're American), letting water into the sink and expecting it to disappear down the drain. It didn't. The drain was still blocked. But the real trouble was that, now, I also had a large quantity of water in my sink. So, I stood and looked at it a while, and that didn't clear it either. Then, I decided to do what every expert plumber does. I read the instructions on the chemical bottle again. It said something like, 'If process does not work, repeat'. So, I made another cup of tea. Eventually, I realised that that wasn't what the manufacturers had in mind, so I went through the whole chemical thing again. Except this time, I first had to remove as much water from the sink as I could. Naturally, the fact that I hadn't managed to remove it all led to even more hisses and gurgles than I experienced the first time, which failed to yield the degree of confidence it had generated in me before. It will come as no surprise to you that the second application had no more success than the first.

So, I decided, in my wisdom, that this chemical was evidently not as powerful as the box indicated, and the manufacturers obviously had not envisaged a blockage as stubborn as mine. Clearly, what was called for was that I use considerably more chemical than advised, for this would surely solve my problem. So, I poured half the bottle down the sink. This time there was real action. Not only did I get hisses and gurgles, I got a thermo-nuclear mushroom cloud wafting out of the waste hole, which proceeded to envelop the kitchen and induce in me a severe coughing attack. I swiftly exited the kitchen, shutting the door firmly behind me and retreated to base camp in the lounge to consider my next move. Unfortunately, I had no access to the kettle to make more tea.

I worked out that I now had two problems. The waste pipe was still blocked and now, I had a cloud of poisonous gas between the sink and me. I was coming to the rather lame conclusion that I really ought to call a plumber. However, in our health-and-safety-conscious society, I was quite certain no one was going to enter my kitchen whilst the mushroom cloud lingered. No one was going to solve that one but me. So, taking a deep breath and holding my nose, I made a swift foray into the kitchen for long enough to open a window and withdraw before having to take a second breath.

I also took a moment more to retrieve the local services directory and, on returning to the lounge, turned up the entry for plumbers. However, by now, I wasn't looking for your average common-or-garden-laid-back-and-not-too-expensive   plumber. Now, I needed an emergency plumber. I dialled, and got a *very* friendly voice at the end of the phone, who informed me that for a mere £27.50 per half hour plus VAT I could expect my plumber to arrive that afternoon. 'Well,' I reasoned, 'it can't take an expert more than an hour to clear this.' (Uh, huh.)

My plumber did indeed turn up that afternoon and he was indeed friendly. He smiled at me most courteously when he told me that he could tell from a momentary glance that he could do nothing for me that day, but would have to return the next morning with special equipment. He positively grinned when he told me the charge for the equipment was an additional £87.50 plus VAT per half hour and he could not predict how long it would take to clear. He then all but guffawed when I told him I had a business meeting the next day and would have to leave him in the flat alone and trust him to charge me the right amount. Yup, this was one friendly plumber all right.

Mr. Smiley returned the next day as promised and quite reasonably, asked that I sign a credit card voucher before he started, since "You might not be back by the time I'm finished." He then mumbled something about taking between half an hour and two hours, but I was too preoccupied with my forthcoming meeting to pay much attention. I asked him to phone me when he was finished so that I knew how much I had spent, and off I drove. It was only when I was an hour away from home that I started to work out the likely cost of solving the problem. £27.50 per half hour for the plumber... £87.50 for the special equipment... that's £115.00 per half hour... plus VAT... that's about £135 per half hour and for two hours... that makes.... Let me see now... OH BROTHER.!

The penny had at last dropped. I'm quick thinking like that. I considered turning the car around and ejecting Mr. Smiley from my flat. No... couldn't do that – I'd miss my meeting and I'd still have a blockage. Anyway, the two hours would be up by the time I got back and he'd have left, so no gain. Considerably less than happy, I proceeded to my appointment. It was a pretty important one, being part of the process of my considering buying into a new business… but I didn't process much of what was said – not even much of what I myself said. My mind was on Mr. Smiley who was racking up costs at the rate of £270.00 per hour, who was about to launch an assault the size of D-Day on my credit card, who was over an hour's drive away and whose phone number I had omitted to take down in my haste both to get my problem solved and to get to my meeting. It was over two and a half hours now… let me see that… OH GOOD GRIEF! I'M RUINED!!

Looking back, what bothered me most was the sense that I was out of control. I had given authority to someone I did not know and whom I had little reason to trust, to charge an unspecified amount to my credit card. My world had departed from my script big time. All I could think about was getting back into my car and heading home at a velocity rather higher than the legal speed limit in a forlorn attempt at damage limitation. You may have lost the presidency, Mr. Nixon, but plumbers could not possibly have cost as much as mine did.

I arrived home about four hours after I'd left, to a bill for £719.66 and a statement that the work was not guaranteed, since there was a fault in my plumbing. Added to that, the chemical I had used had burned its way into the aluminium of the sink and etched a large, indelible black ring around the edges of the waste outlet. I was deeply embarrassed and promised myself I would tell no one of my foolishness that day. But I do experience this rather nagging need to be honest and open, so, I felt in the end, I really had to tell you about it. You do promise not to tell anyone else though, don't you?

Well, the story doesn't end there. Firstly, I had to get someone in to cure the problem of the still-blocked waste pipe and now, also to renew the sink as well. So, I rang someone who had done work for me before and whom I knew I could trust (why didn't I ring him first? Well might you ask. Hey, I've got 20:20 hindsight too, you know). He came later that week, replaced the sink and dislodged the blockage. He told me it was caused by the idiot who had tiled the kitchen for me. Said idiot had apparently washed waterproof grout down the sink which has this irritating habit of setting – even under water. He couldn't understand why anyone who knew about tiling would do anything so dumb. Any decent tiler knows that waterproof grout sets under water. I wasn't going to tell him who tiled the kitchen... but then, I have this irritating need to be honest...

When I had got over the shock and embarrassment of the whole sorry episode, I got to wondering what it was about it that had so disturbed me – particularly, when I was away at my meeting? I thought first, it was the money, for solving a problem I myself had created had cost the best part of a thousand pounds. Now, I don't like to waste money any more than anyone else. But in reality, spending that sum, though irritating, will not be fundamentally life-changing. I had to admit that the real reason for my loss of composure was the sense that I had lost control. And that in turn raises a lot of much more important issues for me – and maybe for you as well – revolving around what we mean by control, and why we feel the need to exercise it.

It seems to me that we wander around the planet in a daze sometimes, thinking it is we ourselves who are in control of our lives – i.e. we think it is we in our conscious minds that determines what happens to us. And yes, we do everything possible to guard against unforeseen eventualities. If we're sensible, we even put cost limits on plumbers and try to avoid self-initiated problems in the first place. But the reality of it is that far more events occur in our lives that are random or out of our conscious control than those which are under our control. Most of the time, we don't notice, for they don't commonly damage what we perceive to be our interests. But occasionally, we are confronted by the fact that we have washed grout down the waste pipes, or failed to limit open-ended costs, or been caught breaking into the Watergate Building in an effort to circumscribe what the public hears about us. And then, as the illusion of control in our world starts to slip away, we begin to react more from unconscious patterns and undisclosed values than from the controlled, public domain reactions we show our conscious minds, or our co-workers, or the nation that elected us.

I rather think we might do better in managing our lives if we started from a presupposition that we cannot consciously control many of the events around us, generated as they are, either randomly or purposefully, by forces other than our conscious minds. My life seems to go much better if I presume a benevolent universe and act accordingly, than if I assume the world is out to get me. When I adopt this approach, I reduce dramatically the sense that I need to control my environment in order to protect myself. Something tells me that in addressing life in this way, I would learn more quickly more of that which I have come here to learn.

Now, where's my drill? I have a few shelves I need to put up this weekend.

16. Tea and Sympathy

I watched you as we talked last night,
wrapping the collar of the darkness round you,
cradling the ecstasy of your pain
like some still-birthed love child,
cold, dead, yet still orchestrating the cries of your passion.

And oh, how the words did fall,
tumbling before you into layered rows,
sealed with the lime of polite euphemism
to conceal your misery behind a wall of cultured gentility.

Somewhere behind that wall, the blood and water flowed,
like the freshly brewed Darjeeling
you poured into Royal Doulton cups.

You thought I would not see you
hanging there in the darkness,
hammering nails of despair
through hands exhausted from self-flagellation,
thrusting that spear of piteous self-loathing
into the soft yielding flesh of your own credulity.

Your blood and water redeem nothing.

Crucifixion's long gone out of fashion.
And the Darjeeling's grown cold in the bone china cups.

17. Emmie

If I saw a face like mine, I'd scream too.

Emmie

I guess the subject first arose, as so much does, because of my consciousness of my hearing loss. My friend Caroline and I were having dinner in a Thai restaurant on the edge of the Forest. I'd already chosen the table and which seat I wanted me to sit in and her to sit in, so as to make it easier for me to lip read her, and I found myself apologising for moving my chair closer as we settled down to the conversation. I thought I was making something of a spectacle of myself and that embarrasses me. Caroline said something along the lines of, "Oh, you've got nothing to worry about, you should imagine what it was like to be with Emmie."

As she spoke, a broad smile stole across her face as she enjoyed the memories of Emmie, their times together flooding back to her. So, now, I was intrigued, and nothing short of a full explanation would satisfy my curiosity. Caroline settled into a story that lasted over into a second evening and which gave me considerable thought in connection with... oh well, let me just tell the story and you'll get the point.

Emmie was cousin to Caroline's father, making her Caroline's own first cousin once removed. A generation back before that, two cousins from the same family had fallen in love and decided to marry. Their relatives were set against the union and warned Emmie's parents that because of proximity of the bloodlines, they might produce abnormal children. But for most of us – particularly, when we are young – when romantic love arrives, rationality and risk are bundled out of the emergency exit to permit that delicious preoccupation with the beloved to take centre stage.

Emmie's parents married and produced in due course a first, perfectly normal child. But when Emmie and her twin arrived, they were both markedly Down's Syndrome. In keeping with medical opinion of the time, neither twin was expected to live long. But by the time Caroline herself arrived into the family, Emmie had reached adulthood. We can only speculate as to what experiences she and those close to her passed through during her childhood and teenage years. For Emmie had chosen to come into the world with a club foot, a hunched back and facial features so out of the ordinary that small children who had not known her from birth were prone to bursting into tears at the sight of her. To face others' reactions to a visible disability or disfigurement in adulthood seems to me to be one of the most challenging experiences we can give ourselves as part of a life contract. To think of those who do so as they pass through the taunts and jeers of childhood fills me with awe and empathy and respect for anyone who makes that choice as part of their contract.

By the time Caroline knew her, Emmie was an adult, though in intellect and emotion she was a child locked into an adult body. Being a child herself in all but body, she was interested in other children and enjoyed being around them. So, she visited Caroline's family often in their home on an open-plan estate where all the children played together. She would arrive on the bus and shuffle in her halting gait from bus stop to house, bent over at the shoulder and dragging a club foot behind her. Emmie was used to it by then, of course, but her appearance in an area where she was unknown made children scream and adults turn away in embarrassment. It was hardly surprising that the first impression the local children had of Emmie was as strange and different and frightening. But with a heart that I can only wonder at, she took the reactions in her stride and continued to visit week by week, for she loved Caroline and shared with her a love of pop music. Each Saturday, they took the bus into town together where, ignoring the stares and the fear on the faces of the onlookers, they would make an almost ritualistic round of the record shops, for Emmie would usually have just enough money to buy one record. But the lady was no fool. Her money was enough to entitle her and her companions to go into each of the music shops and listen on the headphones to several new releases before moving on without actually buying, only to repeat the process all around town. Eventually, towards the end of the day, some hit parade latest would catch her fancy and she would finally part with the money that had been their passport to a full day of entertainment. Then, they would return home by the same bus to play the new acquisition on the family record player, swaying and dancing together until the light began to fail and it was time for Emmie to catch the bus home again.

Each time she showed herself in public, on each occasion she got onto a bus or walked down a street, Emmie would run the gauntlet of revulsion and fear and mockery that those unfamiliar with her would gracelessly bestow upon her. Each time she reacted to the negativity and aggression, as would any child, with pain and with tears.

So, what was it about Emmie that made her pick herself up from each repeated painful experience to face it again on the next occasion on which she exposed herself? Perhaps it was as Caroline thinks, that she had known nothing else since birth; that she accepted the world around her and its reactions to her, positive or negative, without question. Perhaps for Emmie, that was simply the way things were. If you felt pain, physical or emotional, you cried. If you felt pleasure or joy, you smiled and you laughed. And for those of us prone to analysing and seeking to understand the world around us, it seems to me worthwhile to stop and ponder a while on the Emmies of this life and how sensitive to the Tao they must really be. For Emmie accepted the world the way it was and surfed the energy waves as they broke about her without questioning the morality of it all. Therein, lies deep learning.

Taoism is founded upon a text written by Lao Tzu around four thousand years BCE. The title of the text, the "Tao Te Ching", translates literally as "The Way Things Are". That simple acceptance by Emmie of the way things are led to a remarkable change on the part of those who got to know her. For as her visits to Caroline's home became regular, the neighbourhood children grew used to Emmie. Familiarity led to a sense of safety. Safety led to curiosity. And curiosity led to affection, such that as she got off the bus each day, the cry would go up, "Here's Emmie!" and the children would rush to the bus stop to walk with her as far as Caroline's house, not in fear or mockery, but in genuine affection. Such affection is only possible for us to hold as we start to perceive another person's energy beyond their appearance, to begin to know the spirit that lies within the physical form. Then it was that Emmie knew joy and pleasure and laughter, accepting it as readily as she accepted pain and fear and aggression. It was all part of the same energy, the same Tao that she had come here to experience.

Of course, as Caroline grew up, to all practical purposes, Emmie could not. As Caroline reached her teenage preoccupations with boys and O levels, the visits from Emmie grew less frequent. Caroline reached adulthood, married and had two sons. Each of them knew Emmie from birth and accepted her as part of their environment in much the same way as Emmie accepted the reactions of others as part of hers. But Caroline's third child, a daughter, was born after she and her family had left the area, so she was three years old when she saw Emmie for the first time. And as Emmie was used to experiencing, upon seeing her at their first meeting, the child cried from fear. Naturally, Caroline was sad and embarrassed at her daughter's reaction. But though Emmie did not have the sophistication to express herself well, she conveyed to Caroline through her speech impediment and her fast, clipped way of talking, a sense to the effect, "Well, if I saw a face like mine, I'd scream too."

For Emmie, there were no superego or false ego issues. She was simply who she was, and people loved her or feared her for it, as they chose. She had no cause to project any different an image to the outside than the reality she held on the inside. She was simply Emmie.

I, of course, never met Emmie, who died in her forties over thirty years ago. But her life and her learning have influenced me, making me aware once again of the importance of being who I am, with all of my strengths and weaknesses, all my virtues and vices, simply permitting the reality of my identity to be open to the world with no false ego impositions placed upon it for fear of how the world would react to the reality that is me.

And Emmie has reminded me of one more thing. In the words I saw written on the Internet some time ago: "Our perception of beauty indicates how close to the centre of the energy we really are."

18. Why Men Kill

Some men, they kill for power,
Some men kill for belief,
Some kill for retribution,
Some kill to find relief.
Some men will kill from anger,
Some kill to be alone,
And those that kill, when wracked by guilt,
Are unable to atone.

Some sacrifice to dark-eyed gods,
Some men, they kill for treasure.
Some kill to save their shanty homes.
And some will kill for pleasure.

Some kill for cause of evil,
Some kill to dominate.
Some kill, they think, for righteousness,
Some kill because they hate.

Some kill for cause of pointless theft.
Some kill, just to abuse.
Some justify their killing.
Some offer no excuse.

Some hear demonic voices,
Instructions from above.
Some kill from blind obsession,
But no man kills for love.

Men kill for many reasons,
But this the lie dispels:
For all men who have ever killed
Find they have killed themselves.

19. I Shall Tear Down My Barns

I was walking down the high street in The Town this morning and passed the estate agent through which I bought my apartment. There it was in the window with a big proud 'SOLD' stamped across it diagonally in red. I bought it seven months ago, so, though I'm not complaining, I think he must be short of business. I looked at the asking price and raised my chin a little as a shaft of smug self-satisfaction seeped into my smile. Through judicious buying and artful renovation, it is now worth £xxx and I've made a whopping gain of £yyy.

Of course, people are doing it pretty much all over the country, aren't they? If you were born at the right time to ride a rising market and managed to persuade a profit-hungry lender to advance you more than you sensibly should have borrowed, you too could have become obsessed with the pernicious fiction that lies in the financial value of residential accommodation. You too would have all you needed to feel egoistically superior to the rest of the human race. You too could drive a Mercedes-Benz to make amends to all your friends who drive Porsches, as the song goes. Never mind the kids whose only option is renting at stratospheric rates. Never mind that the average age of first-time buyers has now reached 35. Never mind the distraught grandparents who feel obliged to take out equity release mortgages to give their grandchildren a chance to get on to the house ladder to the stars.

Never mind those who can't; whose offspring will never have a prayer of owning their own home.

Am I being harsh? If so, it is with me, not with you. As I was nearing the end of my apartment renovation, I did consider seriously continuing on to another in order to make money on it. And then, there might have been another. And another. Yes, I could once again have become rich beyond the dreams of avaricious folly. But as Matt and I took our morning walk around the recreation ground, I found myself asking why I would do that. To accumulate wealth? To boost my ego? To try to replicate the past in a doomed bid to outrun my own ageing? Because I can?

It was then, I got to asking myself, '*What exactly is the most precious resource I have right now?*' And the answer that came back wasn't money. In saying this, I do not mean to be dismissive of the many, many people who simply do not have enough to put a proper meal on the table or glue a decent life together. But the answer I got back was 'time'. And so I asked myself how I wanted to expend that inestimably valuable and oh, so rapidly diminishing resource.

And that vision appeared that sometimes comes to me – the one of my guide leaning nonchalantly against the wall, legs crossed, arms folded (though sometimes, he has his hands in his pockets) whistling up into the air with a wry smile on his face. When I looked at him enquiringly he said, "Sure! Of course you can go do that again, if you *want* to; if you really *need* to. You can repeat the egocentric pattern as many times over as many lifetimes as you need to. But it's not what you came here for. It's not in your life plan. It's not in your contract." I looked back over the cycles of this lifetime, at the motivators that have driven me to expend my time as I have chosen to, for I have always had a choice. And I found them to be far more concerned with bolstering my ego, and with gaining what I believed to be the admiration and esteem of others (God only knows who these 'others' were and whether they ever did esteem me).

So, this time, I chose different.

Counterintuitive? You bet! For I have become habitual in seeing profit potential, in spying a chance to attract financial energy towards me, and I think it's fair to say that I am very, very good at it. Regrettably, I have not been as good at assessing the opportunity cost of the time expended in taking those opportunities, the stress of the emotional incongruency I have imposed upon myself in so doing. And I can only speculate on where I might now be on this rocky road to enlightenment that we all tread, knowingly or not, if I had made other choices.

Thus, as I approach 60 years of age (a watershed birthday, they tell me), I am addressing the question of what I shall do with my elder days. What a temptation there is to ignore the passing of the years, to fool myself into believing that this lifetime is not finite. Such a belief would incline me to perpetuate my wealth building – to 'tear down my barns and build greater,' as my friend Jesus put it in a story he told some years ago.

The ostensibly opposite temptation is to live for memory in an *'Ah, those were the days'* style. I could relive my moments of greatness. If there truly were any, that is. Were there? Were there really? Or were there simply those days in the self-promoted limelight, where the egos jostle for position and envious eyes survey a moment's passing notoriety? I do value my experiences and would not change any of them. But I do not plan to live for the memory of them. Memory is the journey I have already lived; the learning that is gained and integrated. Guided exploration of the unknown is the journey yet to come; the learning yet to be derived.

And perhaps in so journeying, I shall share a little learning along the way: not to seek ivy accolades, but simply as my friend

Rj (www.sweepingsounds.com) puts it to me, "because gifts should be shared".

So, though my barns have been torn down (and how that came about is a subject we might explore another day) I do not think I shall build greater, merely to fill my days with stress and incongruence. My friend Jesus was assuredly right when he spoke of the rich fool's soul being required of him. The man was not to know he would have to account for himself that very night.

I do not know when I shall have to give an account for the life I have lived, but I'm quite certain I will have to do so. And I also know I am nearly 60 years closer to the accounting reference date than I was when I started this journey. To whom shall I be accounting? Well, there are many different views on that question, but account I know, I shall – and perhaps account particularly for the choices I make in these latter days of quieter thought and deeper travel. When I give that account, I do not want to find myself saying, *'Well, yes, I did come to see the waste of time that resource accumulation is, but it gave me such an ego boost I carried on.'* I don't know if I will have a tail then, but if I do, it will assuredly have to be placed well between my legs.

The Buddha is reputed to have said that in the end only three things will matter: how much you loved, how gently you lived and how graciously you gave up the things that were not meant for you. Instead of resource building, I am thinking to prioritise meditation, learning and growth; and perhaps also, a little gift sharing. For Rj is so right. Gifts should be shared.

20. Where's My Phone?

And we are but flying fish,
breaking the surface for a moment,
to bask in the reflected glory
of a transient elevation.

What's your reaction when you lose something important? It used to throw me into an abject panic as I considered the potential consequences of my loss, the ramifications sometimes seeming well beyond the rational. I look back now and observe with some amusement how welded I have been to my plans for my life, how difficult it has been to consider possibilities outside of the planned.

Yet, I observe now that whether I ever recovered those seeming lost items or not, life carried on regardless. If they were lost forever, I made an adjustment, however initially painful the reordering of my myopic little world, and carried on with a new plan, oblivious to the fallibility of the planning process itself.

With a little more learning behind me, when I mislay something significant now, I am more inclined to smile. For I have come to understand that a major loss will commonly result in an opportunity for intervention from my angels, a learning opportunity, a chance to grow as a result of the divestment of what I no longer need but have kept out of habit, or sometimes all three.

So, when on Sunday evening, shortly before bedtime, I discovered that my mobile phone was missing, the loss itself felt auspicious and I knew something would likely happen that mattered more than the loss itself.

I first searched my flat, checking every possible location in which I might absent-mindedly have put it down or perhaps dropped it (yeah, I do that occasionally, you know), but the search yielded nothing. All the items that I carry with my phone – my keys, my wallet – were sitting quietly where they were supposed to be. All smiled at me questioningly. They evidently knew what was afoot. No one had taken the time to tell me though.

So, I told a few people by e-mail that the misplacement would mean no text communication until the phone or the reason for its absence surfaced. Then, I asked my angels to help me find it. The phone did not appear. Then, I realised I'd made the wrong request of my angels (I generally find I have to be specific in my requests – for they are inclined to respond to the request I have made, not the one I meant to make – funny that, huh?). "Ok, angels," I said, "Please, show me where my phone is." I stopped looking and waited for the answer to surface through my unconscious into my conscious mind in the normal way. I knew it would come.

Only it didn't.

No answer, no phone, no intervention.

Unruffled, I smiled again. "All is well in my world," I found myself responding to a well-meaning sympathiser. But sympathy is rarely useful. "All is as it should be in the moment." And then, I went to bed and slept soundly, just after Matt walked all over me for his night-time cuddle, reminding me of what really matters in my world.

I rose up into consciousness the next morning, aware that

some sort of action would be necessary. The semi-conscious state, that space we cross from sleep to wakefulness, is enormously useful, I find, for creative thought, for active engagement with my guides and angels; but not it seems, for locating misplaced mobile phones.

I did recall the last place I thought I remembered using it though – a dog-friendly café in Lyndhurst where we had stopped the previous afternoon after walking in the Forest. I decided it must be there. But I wake early – too early for the average café to be open – and there was no point in rushing off. So, after Matt's walk we set out to drive back to Lyndhurst where we would join the early risers of the locality in Costa – the only café I know that keeps (almost) the same hours as I do.

And as I drove, I meditated on how far my role models went out of their way to divest themselves of distractions in the pursuit of their life purposes – The Christ, who, so far as we know, never wrote so much as a single book; Gandhi, who eventually owned nothing and dressed in nothing but a homespun loin cloth; Mother (now Saint) Teresa, who discarded all that she might embrace the discarded. And I thought about what a good opportunity this loss might afford to tread in some of the footsteps they left in the sand for me to follow.

We arrived at Costa (I do so love that coffee – for now, anyway) and I read the newspaper, as from habit, I do all too often. It told me of a world of pain and negativity – the vast sea of souls washing into Europe from Africa and the Middle East fleeing terrorists hell-bent on pursing them and us and me with their particular vile brand of odious pestiferousness. I read of the manipulation of millions in the power struggle of elites that is the UK referendum. I read of the emotional opportunism and intellectual poverty of those battling to be the next president of the United States of America. And I contrasted all that with the warm-heartedness and love I perpetually encounter amongst those I engage with on social media, children of light who seek the light. And I resolved to read the news a little less, and meditate a little more in pursuit of my own life purpose.

Then, it was time to go to the café where I would retrieve my misplaced phone that I was confident would be in the possession of the proprietor, whom I would thank with a sheepish smile.

Only I didn't. Because there was a hastily handwritten sign on the door that said 'Closed today for personal emergency. Sorry for any inconvenience.'

I giggled.

Not at the poor proprietor who had an emergency to deal with, but at myself for my presumptuousness. It was then in my mind's eye that I saw a picture of my guide leaning nonchalantly against the wall whistling. And I blessed him for the opportunity not to take myself too seriously and for the certainty that something wonderful was about to happen.

But my phone did not appear.

So, I thought it a good idea to drive to Tesco, my airtime supplier, and have the service cut off in case someone was phoning Kuala Lumpur at my expense (how protective of my money I still am, how far I still have to go in following the divestment examples of my role models). As we arrived in the town, driving past my own flat and on to Tesco, it came.

Not in a whirlwind, not in a fire, but in a voice that was not mine, yet not, not mine. A statement of such profundity I failed initially to appreciate its significance.

"I am done with experiencing my being negatively," came the sentence. I noted it, a very particular and unusual form of words. But I did not understand it.

We drove on to Tesco, had the account switched onto a new SIM card and checked that the phone had not been operated since the last time I remember using it. Then, I drove home, still oblivious to the consequence and meaning of the tsunami that had just washed over me.

Arriving home, I took out a CD of Tibetan singing bowls that I had bought the previous day in a mind body spirit fayre in Lyndhurst, recorded by Ven. Chris Burrows. I had taken a chance on buying it, knowing that even if I could not hear the note of some of the bowls, I would still feel the vibrations. And, as I walked into the study to put the CD case on my desk, I stopped.

It was there; under my chair. I stood in the doorway and looked at it not knowing what to do, frozen in incredulity. The little black object that contains so much of my life and ability to communicate lay on the floor directly under my chair.

Now, you'll maybe say, as I did, momentarily, "It was always there. You just didn't see it... somehow... for some reason."

And maybe, you'd be right. And maybe, the astonishing significance lies in the 'somehow... for some reason'.

And maybe, you'd not be right. And maybe, it had not been there, but now it was.

Because whether you're right, or whether you're wrong, it hit me just the same. With the full force of that delayed tsunami, it hit.

The koan, the gongan nature of the event was beyond mistaking. The energy of its intervention threw me full force against the inestimable magnitude of that life-changing statement, "I am done with experiencing my being negatively," and in that moment came the awareness of the beyond-identity, cascading down, and in and up and out, blinding in its force of revelation. Confronting me with the new reality – that I am not an individual being, that the I of the me is not a sole inhabitant of my body, that our soul connection goes inestimably beyond the individuality of my perception, that all the protectiveness I have built up, the unrecognised negative on which I have built my ramparts, the false belief that others are different, separate, threatening, dangerous, other in their otherness, in their unconnect.

All melted in the heat of the light. And I howled to heaven. And I wept and I laughed. A Holy Spirit baptism in which I poured out in the tongues of men and angels in reverence to and declaration of the revelation and to the light and the grace and the love of enlightenment.

Have you seen it yet? Have you seen it in this lifetime, I mean? For we all do see it when we return and before we come again. When we slide back into the arms of God, we know the join-edness of unified integration. The sea of souls is one sea.

21. It's My Right

1984
In San Ysidro, Huberty
Took 21 in McDonald's.
Most hadn't got to puberty
Which really pissed off Ronald.
And I thought: "The world is dangerous!"
Cos the killing had begun
So, I exercised my A2 rights
And bought myself a gun.

1986
In Oklahoma Pat Sherrill
Killed 14 post guys dead.
Then, turned his gun the other way
And shot himself in the head.
I thought: "This world's so dangerous!
And I don't get too much fun."
So, I exercised my A2 rights
And bought another gun.

1991
It was back in 1991
Ol' Georgie crashed his truck.

Then, he turned his gun on 23.
Don't some folks get bad luck?
And I thought, "This world's real dangerous."
Cos the killing wasn't done.
So, I exercised my A2 rights
And bought me 3 more guns.

2012
In Sandy Hook, he took a look
And gunned down 20 babies,
And the politicians yelled out loud.
Said "Gun Control? Yeah, maybe."
Now, I knew the world was dangerous,
So, not to be outdone
I exercised my A2 rights
And bought me 5 more guns.

2016
In Pulse, he took out 49
But they don't count. No Way!
Cos they was in a nightclub
And all them boys was gay.
So, I thought the Gays and Liberals
Might rig the vote machines.
And I exercised my A2 rights
And bought AR15s.

2017
In Sutherland it was 26
But one of 'em don't count.
It was just an unborn baby –
I demanded they re-count.

And I thought that them Pro-Lifers
Could start to get much tougher.
So, I bought another A15
In a really pretty colour.

2018
In Parkland, 17 went down,
That's adults and the kids,
While the Deputy just stood outside,
And he might as well have hid.
So, I knew the law would not protect,
Cos Trump, he loads and locks.
So, I exercised my A2 rights,
Bought 20 new bump stocks.

We'll load them up with all the toys
And go and have some fun.
We'll pack the Hummer to the brim
And march on Washington.
There's 265 million guns out there
And if they try to take 'em off us,
We'll set 'em up at Lincoln's feet
And shoot 'em out of office.
So, now we have a civil war
And yeah, it's touched my life.
Last night, they bombed us in our house
And the bastards got my wife.
So, we'll mourn her for at least a day
And read out her last rites.
But it really doesn't matter.
I've still got my A2 rights.

22. Bridges Over Troubled Waters

Like a bridge over troubled water
I will lay me down

Paul Simon

I talk a great deal over the Internet. As a hearing-disabled person, I have found it a 'level playing field', so to speak, in conversations with hearing people. However, the real reason I continue to do so is that I find it a fascinating place to meet people, since all of humanity seems to be represented there. People of all nations, all beliefs, all persuasions come together with an endless number of personal agendas and intentions. I find that, in many cases, people are prepared to talk more openly and at a deeper level than they would normally do if I were to meet them in person. That may be attributable to the safety that lies in the anonymity of the medium and the fact that you are talking to complete strangers who have no access to the rest of your life. You know that at a touch of a button you can end the conversation and walk away from the screen without further involvement, should you wish to do so. That makes it, at one level, a very safe place to express yourself. At other levels, it can be very dangerous, as a result of dishonesty. But nevertheless, I find it fascinating when I get into conversations where people are willing to disclose more of their real selves than they would in the outside world, where they allow me in behind the veneer that virtually all of us use to project an image in social contexts.

I want to tell you about one conversation I had recently. It was with a lady I shall call Sarah, who lives in London. Sarah's marriage ended three years ago, and she is left living with her five-year-old son in somewhat complex emotional circumstances. Our conversations explored some themes around the patterns we all run in our lives and why they impact upon our relationships – sometimes disastrously. I promise, I will get to that conversation in due course, but if this Learning is to make proper sense to you, and is to deliver the energy I intend it to, I need to fill you in on another line of personal thinking that has been running for me for some time now. Bear with me – as always, we will get to the point, eventually.

Years ago, when my family was young, we lived in Cardiff, South Wales. We had many friends in London whom we used to visit frequently, and that required that we take the M4 motorway over the first River Severn road bridge. Now, I have always had a bit of a thing about engineering structures. Maybe I was a pyramid builder in a former lifetime, or maybe I am just a frustrated architect at heart. Who knows? Whatever the reason, though, I am fascinated by the elegance of engineering constructions, and the Severn Bridge is one that I particularly enjoyed. So often would I comment on it as we passed over it, that eventually, the kids got to parodying my predictable responses. As the bridge came into sight, a chorus would emanate from the back seat of the car in mock admiration along the lines of "Just look at that wonder of modern engineering... beautiful... stunning... remarkable." Inevitably, this would be followed by a series of not terribly well concealed giggles. Yeah, they had me down to a 'T' – but it didn't stop me admiring man-made structures for the elegance in their design and the aesthetic appeal of their soaring towers, and for the sheer nobility of their imposing presence.

You see, on looking at such structures, I see not only the physical beauty (and ok, beauty is in the eye of the beholder) but also the design elegance of the thought that has gone into such edifices. I think about the teams of engineers and draughtspeople running calculations on design capacities and stress levels. I visualise them considering the numbers of people who will use a bridge, or a building, or a motorway. I think of them working out the environmental stress factors that such creations will have to endure with regard to weather conditions, vibrations, moisture content of the air, sunlight and numerous other factors of which I, as a layman, have no knowledge. In thinking through such matters, I am reminded that an engineering structure is not simply a single entity. In a very real sense, it is a system – a combination of elements that are drawn together in congruence to create a whole that is more valuable than the sum of the parts could ever be. And when I think of such systems, I am also deeply conscious that they have a design capacity. That capacity refers not only to the level of utilisation the system is expected to bear, but also the circumstantial conditions it is expected to withstand – the predictable environmental factors of vibration and moisture that stress the system, within its design capacity.

Of course, sometimes the engineers get it wrong and the system behaves in ways that were not anticipated. Hence, for example, when the Millennium Bridge in London was opened for pedestrian traffic only, it was discovered within a very short time that the people walking across it were causing the bridge to vibrate and sway. Not surprisingly, it was very quickly closed whilst some red-faced designers oversaw modifications that counteracted the problem. I'm glad to say that bridge was reopened relatively quickly with no damage done and no one harmed. But where, over a sustained period, systems are stressed beyond their design capacity, they will typically show signs of that stress by way of lingering weaknesses in the structure.

Sometimes, even when designed without error, engineering systems are subjected to levels of stress that were not anticipated by the designers. The memory that lingers with me most in this context is of the disastrous damage done to the freeways during the San Francisco earthquake of 1989. I had little connection with the USA at the time, but still remember the TV pictures showing sections of freeway twisted into grotesque parodies of their elegant former selves by the intolerable levels of stress placed upon them. I recall in particular, the appalling sight of the upper section of a double-deck freeway that simply collapsed onto the lower section, trapping and crushing numerous vehicles and their passengers between the two levels of the road. The scars on the lives of the survivors and others affected will perhaps never fully heal. The memory will linger even with long-distance observers for decades.

The conclusion from all of this is simple: systems have a design capacity. If you exceed the levels of stress they were intended to take, they will behave in ways you did not plan. Apply enough pressure over and above their design capacity and they will malfunction and eventually tear themselves apart.

So why do I tell you all this? Because it is not only engineering systems that have a design capacity. All systems do. Just like engineering systems, all other systems will malfunction if subjected to excess stress levels for long enough. They will bear the marks and weaknesses of such excess stress indefinitely. And all systems will eventually collapse when subjected to too much excess pressure for too long.

What do I mean by other systems? Well, certainly, economic and political systems will behave in this way, as will social systems, and those social systems include relationships such as marriages. Equally significantly, biological systems, psychological and perhaps even spiritual systems behave in the same way when subjected to intolerable stress levels – and here I am talking about such bio-psycho-spiritual systems as human beings.

We, too, are systems ourselves. We function within systems, for the universe is interrelated, or, if you will, systemic. And like all other systems, our personal system has a design capacity, and our relationship systems with other humans have a design capacity. If we exceed the stress tolerance levels of a system, be it human or social, the system will malfunction and eventually break down. In the worst of cases, the system will tear itself apart under the intolerable levels of stress.

So what does all this have to do with Sarah and my conversations with her on the Internet? Well, as I was saying earlier on, Sarah lives in the East End of London, close to her roots (she is an East Ender born to a Jewish father and a gentile mother so, as she pointed out to me, she is rejected as Jewish by the Jews and considered as Jewish by the gentiles). What makes it harder is that Sarah comes from a holocaust family. Her father was German, the only family member of his generation to escape the concentration camps. Now, perhaps you begin to see where this is going. If you stress a system beyond its design capacity, it falters, behaving in ways in which it was not designed to behave and may eventually self-destruct. But if the system does survive, the stress marks remain, affecting the performance of the system ever after.

One of the ways we human systems reflect our stress marks is in our subsequent behavioural patterns. In an oft-quoted passage, The book of Jeremiah in the Bible talks of the fathers eating sour grapes and the teeth of the children being set on edge. It also says that that "the sins of the fathers are visited upon the children unto the third and fourth generation". These postulates do not appear for literary emphasis or religious influence. They are simply statements of how the systems that we are, function inherently. Where my parents were stressed beyond their design capacity, they crystallised the stress lines into behavioural patterns that affected me. I, in my turn, reflected my responses to their expression of their fault lines into my own behavioural patterns that have gone on to affect my life. To those patterns, I have added my own responses to the stresses I have suffered beyond my design capacity. These, in my turn, I have conveyed in my own patterns to my children, who themselves will have developed behavioural patterns of their own in response, in part, to my ways of being. The social system that is the family is highly effective in handing down the stress marks and fault-line cracks of the system from generation to generation. The sins of the fathers – and the mothers too, for that matter – are indeed visited unfailingly upon the children.

However bad I might be tempted to think my own circumstances have been, I acknowledge that the stresses that have influenced Sarah's family and Sarah herself are far more profound than any I have faced so far in this lifetime. Sarah's father dealt with the horrors of his circumstances by withdrawing emotionally. Sarah, not surprisingly, has been left with anger and hatred and a sense of disapproval that she has as yet been unable to throw off. In her turn, it has translated into unhelpful behavioural patterns she applies in her own life.

Sarah has sought out abusive men with whom to enter into relationships. She has accepted sexual abuse as the norm. Her problem, as she articulates it, is that she then is prone to falling in love with the men she is with and as a consequence wants the abuse to stop. Her partners run their patterns for their own reasons and their own experiences, but nothing in Sarah's changed expectations upon falling in love is ever enough to make them change their behaviour towards her. For the abuse in their own lives is rooted too deep to be able to be easily altered. And so the merry-go-round goes on.

Sarah entered into one such relationship some years ago, fell in love and got married. She and Dave lived well enough together for five years until Sarah became pregnant. Upon the birth of their son, "something clicked in Dave" in her words, and he announced he was gay and needed daily gay sex. At the same time, he continued to demand daily sadomasochistic sex from Sarah, immediately following her returning home with her new baby. Quite naturally, all this put the marriage under intolerable stress, for Sarah could not understand how someone she loved could subject her to such pain. Dave announced if he could not have his daily dose of s-m sex he was leaving; which he duly did, having left a previous wife in precisely analogous circumstances some five years prior to marrying Sarah. According to Dave, he does not run patterns, he just suffers coincidences.

It would be an understatement to say that Sarah is angry with Dave. Dave sees his son periodically but is aware he is missing out on the boy's growing up. Unsurprisingly, Sarah will not have Dave back. She is quite understandably consumed with anger at the way Dave treated her in the weeks following the birth of their son. Though she recognises that Dave is running patterns he cannot control, he has said and done things to her that strike at the heart of her sense of identity. She cannot really understand his behaviour at the emotional level and we cannot easily forgive and let go of what we do not understand. Dave's conduct is unforgivable to her because it affects her view of who and what she is. She holds her anger deeply. It is justified. It is her entitlement and she treasures it close to her heart.

Do I judge her for this? Assuredly not. I simply observe that this pattern prevents her from exploring what possibility of reconciliation there might be with Dave (who admittedly may not want reconciliation himself) and what benefit there may be to all of them in reconciliation. The stresses and fault-line cracks that both Sarah and Dave carry from past experiences, past generations (and perhaps past lifetimes) have stressed the system of their marriage so excessively that it has broken down.

The deeper we are hurt, the closer the hurt comes to our sense of identity, the less forgiving we can be – particularly, if the hurt has raised uneasy possibilities about ourselves that we secretly suspect may be true, but that we are too afraid to explore. It is, for many of us, easier to cover up that uneasiness with the anger we justly carry at the abuse to which we have been subjected, than it is to explore such dangerous possibilities concerning who and what we fear we might be.

Sarah might acknowledge intellectually that Dave was unmanageably stressed in those weeks after the birth of their son by forces he could not understand or control. She may have enough awareness to realise that it is misunderstood and alterable patterns of behaviour that have placed her family in the position they are in. But it is too scary, too risky, to look openly inside herself for long enough to consider the demon she fears lies within, the demon that screams her unacceptability in her face, whose existence Dave's abuse has forced some part of her to confront. She must deny the existence of the demon, stuff him back in the box, sit on it and padlock it shut. Because to look at that demon risks finding Dave and her worst fears about herself are right – that she is unacceptable, invalid and lacking the right to exist. To face the danger of looking inherently requires rejection of Dave, rejection of what she does not understand, rejection of what she fears.

The sadness of this is that were she to confront the demon,

she would discover he is made of ice. She could watch him melt, as she whispers to herself the words of understanding that apply to her own and everyone else's patterns, that "the fathers have eaten sour grapes and the teeth of the children are set on edge"; that her unspoken terror that she may be worthless emanates from patterns in her parents conveyed to her in childhood. Such an understanding would yield options she does not have open to her at present – such as seeking reconciliation, such as letting go of her anger and moving forward, if she did not choose reconciliation.

Sarah may be angry with me when she reads this. She will probably disagree with what I'm saying. She may rightly feel that I am some anonymous Internet amateur psychologist with absolutely no understanding of her circumstances at all and no right to vent my opinion of her private matters on paper. Perhaps she is right and perhaps there is no hope for her marriage now, anyway.

But there is one thing I do know. It comes from looking into my own soul and it is this: we carry around with us our patterns and our ice-demons until such time as we are willing to confront them; until we are willing to risk the possibility of finding that they may indeed be real, which would mean that what little self-worth we have been able to muster over the years is invalid; that we have no right to exist in a world that would be perfect without us. Yet, it is in the very willingness to risk this confrontation that we see as so dangerous, that we are able to unmask the ice-demons and the patterns for what they are, and to judge them as unfounded and unhelpful. For the key lies not in what another thinks of us, no matter how highly we once esteemed them. It lies in what we think of ourselves. And it is only by being willing to look at ourselves that we can acknowledge the reasons for our patterns, change the ones that were unhelpful and melt the ice-demon in the sunlight of mature, considered evaluation. Until we do, our system will continue to be incapable of dealing with excess stress which threatens our identity and our inherent right to exist, especially around the fault-line cracks handed down from generation to generation. In the systemic nature of the universe in which we live, the sins of the fathers will continue to be visited upon the children unto the third and fourth generation.

But if we do reach the point of being willing to unpadlock the box and confront the ice-demons – and it takes an effort of unparalleled bravery to do so – they melt into the torrid waters boiling below us, such that those waters themselves become a little less troubled. We begin to erect those elegantly engineered bridges of self-confidence that span the chasms to lands of serenity and contentment. We at last start to move forward in our lives and find peace. Ultimately, the only person who can engineer the laying down of a bridge over your own troubled waters is you.

Postscript.

Well, I showed the draft of this Learning to Sarah, and sought her permission to put it into the public domain. She wasn't angry. Apart from the correction of some minor factual inaccuracies, she was pretty much in agreement with what you have read here. She has asked for a hard copy to show her psychologist, which of course I shall send her.

But what really arrested me in her response was that, though 'Sarah' is just a name I chose randomly to anonymise the piece, it turns out to be the identity she mostly uses for talking over the Internet. And she keeps her own writings about herself in a file. The file is called 'Sail on Silver Girl'.

Don't you just love synchronicity?

23. Madonna of All Hallows

And would you rule the midnight hour?
Feigned self-confidence
grasps vainly at elusive echoes of self-worth
that summon you upon the sometime winds of yesterday.
Silently, you smother longing sighs,
bolstering bravado with gaudy neon interjections
and the thrusting heartbeat of the surging crowd.

Somewhere, between the flickering candles of audacious
confidence and the pumpkin shadows of despair, stirs a waking
soul.

Bright-eyed, young and beautiful, exuding sensuality,
you step across my trance to offer me your body
for a few low value notes
and all of my integrity;
a price so far beyond my means.

And was I tempted to caress your flesh?
Momentarily.
But then, the moment fled.
I smiled into your eyes
and complimented you upon your beauty

that will fade so very soon
(where lies longevity, I wonder still, for those who trade upon the transient?).

Yet, after I had walked away, I had repeated cause to think again. With perseverance, it is possible you might have let me touch your soul.
I could have been a conduit to your higher cause.
I would like to be the first to tell you, you are loved.

You are loved.

24. Manic Street Preachers

He stands, black leather bible in hand, between two yellow flags that flap out selectively un-contextualised words of scripture in a manner somehow reminiscent of a pair of oversized budgerigars on steroids.

What I notice first about him is his eyes, his hunted eyes, that belie his purported belief in the message he wants me to hear, leaving me wondering whether he is preaching to my heart or his own. I'm not sure he knows the answer himself. The words pour out at a pace seemingly adopted to prevent the interruption of rational though on his own part, as much as the occasional heckles he periodically attracts from less tolerant watchers than me.

Though I cannot hear his words, the preacher's body language and posture resonate me back across the years. This is a belief set I was taught in my childhood, grew uneasy with in my teens and rejected in my twenties. I could not be more relieved to have left it far behind on my journey. Yet, I seemingly cannot avoid an emotional reaction, as this brand of theology (or is it bigotry? – you tell me) is a close cousin to that on which I was spiritually weaned. Sometimes, my reaction to such messages is uneasy discomfort, re-engendering the latent sense of guilt that his forebears were so good at pouring over my young psyche by the tsunami-load. Sometimes, it is anger, that in a world crying out for enlightenment and love, such men feel the need to terrorise 'sinners' (for which read anyone who believes remotely differently from them) into salvation, by fear of hellfire, damnation and eternal separation from the God I know and love dearly. Most often it is sadness: sadness for him rather than the passers-by that do not listen; sadness for the many, many lifetimes he seemingly will need in order to forgive himself for whatever drives him to externalise his condemnation.

Usually, I pass such people by, minding my own business, for I hold it to be true that the beliefs each of us espouse at any particular moment are a step on the road to enlightenment each must take. Under normal circumstances, it is not for me to intervene in the beliefs of another.

But today is different. Today, our eyes meet. I am, by policy, non-belligerent, non-confrontational. But from this arm-lock of eyes, I know today will be different. His lips move. I do not get what he says first time. I put down my shopping and look at him enquiringly. He repeats. This time, I get it. "Are you saved?" he asks in a threatening semi-whisper. I have a choice. Will I answer? Will I engage on his selected territory? I make my choice.

"Saved from what?" I reply.

And then, the deluge starts. I get some of it. Even in deafness, it's not so hard when you have been familiar with this unremitting flagellation since childhood: saved from my sin for we are all sinners; saved from the sin of eating from the fruit of the tree of knowledge, knowledge that has set me free from his clutches long ago. When I ask him to repeat, he finally gets it. He looks down at Matt who is standing patiently, unaware that he, too, must presumably be a sinner, condemned to eternal separation from God.

There's something to be said for being a dog and having body language as your first language at times like these. The preacher evidently disapproves of deafness as it prevents me from falling at his feet in condemnation for the sin he tells me is killing me. But he doesn't disapprove enough to let me go. And when I mis-hear and ask for clarification he berates me for being witty. "Witty?" I ask his companion in surprise, for today, he is not alone.

"Don't worry," comes the companion's answer, for he is indeed quite companionable. "He's in preaching mode," as if such a modality excuses the preacher's impatient cussedness.

I stand before the ineloquent spew a little longer before I can take no more. I offer a hug, but the preacher will not accept a hug. The companion accepts, so perhaps the exchange is not entirely wasted. "Namaste," I say, hands together in supplication. As I turn to walk away, the words fly past me in an unending stream of condemnation and promises of death in the unquenchable fires of hell.

Walking home, I explore my animated emotions and realise that little has been accomplished other than a temporary disturbance to my own equilibrium. There are still changes to make before I am as grounded in serenity as I wish to be.

Sadly, the preacher has sustained an impression I have gained repeatedly over the years from numerous Christians who regrettably have ranked amongst the most obnoxious, confrontational and deliberately offensive people I have encountered. They worship an intolerant God, these loveless men of a harsher Calvary than the one I know. One step out of line and He condemns you to an eternity of pain and loneliness. Their antidote? Derision, mockery and a megalomanic smug superiority. It seems to me that these self-appointed representatives of God on earth dwell worlds away from the Jesus they purport to follow. Nothing about them endears. I could not conceivably ever wish to emulate them or anything they stand for. I rather think Jesus would have disowned them. Perhaps he still does.

So, I return home to my singing bowls and my meditation and my crystals to re-establish equilibrium.

I have written the preacher a poem. I shall carry a copy and give it to him next time I see him.

Oh My God!

"Repent!" he shouted.

I didn't know what penting was, but I promised there and then, I'd definitely re-do it more in future.

"All ye like sheep have gone astray," he yelled.
I thought of new season's lamb with mint sauce and roast potatoes.

The kingdom of heaven is at hand," he snarled.
I looked at my hands. There was nothing on them, certainly not a kingdom.

"I see you, sinner," he said.
I checked my flies.

"There will be weeping and wailing and gnashing of teeth," he said.
I wiped a tear from my eye and adjusted my dentures.

"What do you worship?" he demanded in a booming voice.

And they all looked at me.

So, I said:

"That's my God standing over there.
My God's the one sweating blood in a lonely garden.
My God's the one carrying a cross up a hill on his back.
My God's the one with twelve-inch thorns crushed down onto his head.
My God's the one stripped naked and nailed up high.
My God's the one who forgives thieves.
My God's the one whose body burned its way through a winding sheet.
My God's the one that Death wasn't strong enough to hold (and believe me, Death's pretty pissed off about that).
My God's the one who kicked an 'effin great boulder out of his way and strode out of his tomb.
My God's the one who forgave every bad or stupid thing I ever did.
And what's more, He doesn't give a toss what you or anyone else thinks of me.

So, that's my God," I said,

"What's yours like?"

25. Murder in the Cathedral

Winston Churchill, I am reliably informed, was not a churchgoer. When pressured by his wife to attend alongside her, his response is said to have been, "Clemmie, you and I are both supporters of the church, but you are a pillar and I am a buttress. You support the church from the inside, I support it from outside." Whether this was merely a convenient turn of phrase for the great statesman to extricate himself from marital strife, or whether he genuinely mean it, who can say?

However, I have a problem of my own with Christianity. My problem lies not in the empty tomb of Christ, but in the cathedral of power that succeeding generations of authoritarian rule-givers have erected over it. This cathedral has been built with impenetrable floors of regulation and with bricks of edict, fabricated steadily over the years into walls of coercive stipulation. It also appears to me that this edifice has not been built true to the head of the corner. The self-aggrandising power-lust of egotistical jerry-builders has led to an inherent instability in the structure. And those Sistinian ceilings, adorned with jewels mined by the hands of the hungry; those ceilings are cracking.

And why? Because at the heart of the structure, there is something missing. A key ingredient has been omitted from the mortar-mix that holds the entire structure together and that ingredient is the blood of love. For an edifice of spiritual power can only be constructed by steady infusions of the blood of love. Yet, the blood of love, integral to a successful mortar-mix that binds in power, has consistently been replaced by a readily available and ostensibly more affordable ingredient.

It is not as if that substitution has been made in the odd batch of mortar, either. Successive generations of construction managers have repeated the same act of folly, time after time, deeming the blood of love to be too costly for this building, choosing instead to squander the construction budget on the adornments of frescoed walls and pain-carved graven images that all carry the same face: the face of self-glorification.

So, instead, the construction managers have specified an alternative ingredient to replace the blood of love, which, though on first glance appears much the same, suffers from a key deficiency: it comes at someone else's cost. But why would they not? After all, once the building is complete, who will know the difference? Who will be able to say that the architect's specification has not been adhered to? Women and men will still come from afar to revere the beauty of the cathedral and applaud the wisdom of the construction managers. No one will ever know the difference, will they?

And thus, the cathedral of self-aggrandisement has been completed with blood. But it is not the blood of Christ, the blood of love, that has moistened the mortar-mix, holding the building firm and true to the design specification of the architect. It is the blood of the weary and the hungry, the soul-lost and the hopeful, who come to the cathedral in search of respite. As they trudge, sole-sore and soul-sore through the doors, ever hopeful of an embrace of selfless love, they find themselves received instead with a bear-hug of demands and requirements, which squeezes the breath of hope out of them, time after time, until hope itself hangs dead, sacrificed upon a crucifix of exploitation.

Yet, all the while, beneath the structure, where no one can see it any more, lies the reason for it all: the tomb. And in that tomb still lies the Shepherd; not an active, death-defying Shepherd, risen to lead his long-lost sheep into the light, but a still-entombed Shepherd, whom the cathedral builders and the building managers and a veritable army of self-declared leaders of the flock simply cannot afford to see break through that concrete floor of catechism.

For, if he were ever to be released, a crucial secret would be out. And that vast flock of blood donors, on whom the whole great structure depends for its continuance, would know that secret and they would stop giving blood to the cathedral managers preferring instead to give it to a risen Shepherd. And this Shepherd, he would use it for life-giving transfusions to the expiring sheep, enabling them to spring back into life and love and the power of spirit they have yet to discover they contain within them.

So, this secret, the secret that is too important to share with the blood donors, what is it? What can it possibly be, that would so put at risk the last remaining stability of the crumbling edifice? It is this: 'Christ in you, the hope of glory.' Not Christ in the church, standing statuesque while self-preferring men and women build powerbases to bolter egos, but Christ *in you*: a heart-changing, revolutionising, life-path-altering Christ; a Christ who stops egotism mid-stride, by laying down self interest in favour of tangible acts of demonstrative love.

Show me this Christ. Show him to me, not in words designed to assert authority over me, in fear that I might otherwise challenge your fragile sense of superiority. Show him to me, not in your surreptitious assessment of how I might advance your agenda of personal achievement. But rather, show him to me by taking the risk of loving me. Show him to me in the genuineness of your smile and in giving me what I need but can never afford to reciprocate. Show me in your kindness that seeks no kindness in return. Show me in your eyes that do not glaze over when I seek to engage you, for from this, I will know that you see me as more than mere donation-fodder.

Show me this Christ when you can embrace an alcohol-dependant woman who has struggled in through the side door of your cathedral, disrupting your prayers with her wails of misery, for maybe then, I will feel able to join you. Show him to me when you kneel before a sexually abused child, who is cowering in the corner behind the hymnals, when you excommunicate his abuser and when you ask this child for his forgiveness. Perhaps then, I shall worship in harmony with you. And show him to me when you wash the bleeding feet of the broken with your tears of heartfelt repentance and dry them with your designer-coiffured hair. Show me when you decide to sell your shares in petrochemical companies that you might buy bread and blankets to feed the poor; when you sell your shares in social media providers so that you can fund the conversion of your empty churches into places where you engage the lonely and embrace the dying. For then, I may be able to stand among you and listen to the words of this Christ who you have, by your acts of love, permitted to rise, unshackled and ungagged from the tomb.

And show him to me, please, when you are willing to hold your august and learned conferences, not in five star hotels in vacation resorts, your expense accounts discharged by the sacrifices of the weary, but in the ruins of bombed-out conference centres in Aleppo and Mosul, where you, too, will sleep in rows of draughty tents alongside the war-weary. And let the subject of those conferences be not ecumenical reconciliation, or whether to accept the otherness of gays, and Goths and tattooed trans. But rather let your podiums ring with advice as to the best way to wind a bandage for the binding of a shrapnel wound, as did a certain Samaritan of your former acquaintance, or upon the subject of which toys might best be gifted to raise smiles in traumatised children who have fled, screaming, from the Sarin shells. Let your break-out rooms focus upon the most effective means of dispensing medicines that prevent camp-born refugee babies from dying of dysentery. Meditate upon the redemption, not of the privileged-born souls of the western wealthy, but of the debts of the poverty-stricken and the hopelessly indebted. And let the lunches at those conferences consist not of designer gourmet dishes. But instead feast yourselves upon bread and water, whilst listening to discourses concerning the feeding of hungry orphans. Then, use the money so saved in the feeding of those orphans who surround such conference centres, begging bowls in hand.

And, oh yes, just one more thing: let the queues for delegate tickets to attend such conferences stretch twice around the world, though the price of admission be eye-wateringly high, paid for by fasting for a week from go-large burgers and latte-to-go service coffee.

However, if, in your status-preoccupied, fear-driven, control-obsessed egotism, you choose instead to murder your Shepherd once again, in an unending death of slow asphyxiation, do not expect me to join the supplications of the sycophants, who mingle within the congregations of the acquiescent. But rather, if you will rather emancipate your Christ, if you will ungag him, I prophecy this: he will send a message from the tomb, a message that is for me and for you and for all of us. It is the same message he has always preached. If you will listen with open hearts and open ears, if you will act upon that message, then, the floor of the cathedral will shake to the march-step of an army of love. And it will shudder and it will crack, as through it soars an emancipated Christ, a Christ who is waiting only for you to release him. And this is the true Christ, the Christ who really is the hope of glory.

Show me this Christ and how could I not embrace him? For this is the Christ I have always known and who has always known me, into whose arms I have always wanted to sink. Who will unshackle this Christ for me, that I, too, might call myself a Christian? Who will remove the gag from his mouth that he may roar out his message again, as many times as we need to hear it, until finally we understand it, finally we believe it to the point where we act upon it.

For the message is this:

By their fruits shall ye know them.

26. Land of Hope and Glory

I'll tell you of a friend of mine,
A lass of long acquaintance.
I've watched her as the years roll by.
Alone, she gets no maintenance.

The social stopped her benefits.
They said she doesn't need them.
Her kids go hungry off to school,
Cos she can't afford to feed them.

They say that she should hold a job.
But who will hold her child?
Should she put him naked on the streets,
Barefoot and running wild?

She does her best to cope alone,
But trying gets her no thanks.
So, she cringes in embarrassment
When queuing in the food banks.

They tell her that she's made her bed
And in it she must lie.
But her children's daddy died today

And she's got no time to cry.

She can't afford to bury him.
He'll find a pauper's grave.
And there'll be no cash for headstones,
Since they say she should have saved.

She'd go back down to Social,
Give them all a bit of lip.
But she's terrified they'll take some more –
They're the ones who cut her PIP.

She's sick with worry from the stress,
She went to get some tablets.
But the doctors wouldn't help her –
Just said to change her habits.

The foreign nurses all went home.
The GPs all retired.
At the mercy of the CQC,
The patients all expired.

The Regulator's in control,
They'll tell you you're defiant.
And when you say you're healing folk,
They'll find you non-compliant.

There's old folk lying in the beds,
They're soaking in their urine,
While the people queue at A&E,
Where there's no one left to cure them.

We're pulling teeth from little kids
So they can raise a smile.
But the only ones left grinning,
Are execs at Tate and Lyle.

The government has got no cash,
They face financial barriers.
Tell that to the kids who die of cold
While you're launching aircraft carriers.

I know we have to have defence
Lest the Russians overrun us.
But it seems to me a huge offence
That hunger walks among us.

Preoccupied with Brexit,
I'll not blame that Mrs May.
But I know we'll find on exit
That it's still the poor who pay.

You say I have no sense of pride?
That the kingdom is united?
But in or out, in the same old way,
It's the weak who'll get exploited.

They tell me that my land of birth's
A land of hope and glory
But the news I read of every day,
It tells a different story.

I'm a caring kind of person,
When the tins get shook I fill them.

So they've got the cash to aid relief –
But the charities rape children.

The DfID, it can't stop this rot?
Can't stop it? Pah! My arse!
When the senior Civil Servants
Fly the world in Business Class?

The kids, they can't afford to buy
A rabbit hutch in London.
As they try to save deposits,
The prices soar above them.

The Fulham Road is paved with gold,
The wealth funds bought out Highbury.
Ferraris crowd out Kensington
And the Oligarchs own Chelsea.

We talk about the need for homes
But we never seem to build them.
Yet the queue is snaking out the door
Of folks who want to fill them.

I'd cast my vote with Labour
But I fear the unions' power.
I still recall the three-day week
With the current off for hours.

Do I write too many verses?
Will you not take time to know?
Go tell the homeless on the streets
Who are dying in the snow.

You say you are superior,
You are a breed apart.
But inside you have an iceberg
Where there should have been a heart.

Your Bitcoins buy you super yachts.
You sail them out to sea.
But there's no room for compassion
In your crypto-currency.

There's work for those that want?
And I'm making too much fuss?
Just go and buy another jet
And screw the rest of us.

27. Lamplighter

On the day before Christmas, I walked through the park in the late afternoon, the snow swirling about me. In my hand I held my lamp, that I might see my way clearly. Out beyond the railings, the merrymakers ebbed and flowed, the music of their happiness carried to me on a chill December wind. They, too, were making their way home, lamps and Christmas gifts in hand.

As I peered through the failing light, before me, I could just make out a figure huddled on a park bench, a woman, drawing her coat collar around her as she shivered, alone in the cold. On the bench beside her lay her lamp, unlit. I approached, concerned she might be in need of assistance.

"Why do you sit here alone in the cold?" I asked.

"I am waiting for the one I love," she answered.

"But why is your lamp unlit?" I asked. "Darkness is about to fall, and you will not be able to see your way home."

"The one I love will light my lamp," she answered. "He is the Lamplighter."

"But there is no need to wait," I responded. "All have light and you can ignite your lamp from the lamp of any other. In fact, if you wish, you are welcome to light your lamp from mine."

"I thank you, but no," she answered. "The one I love is the Lamplighter and I will accept only his light to light my lamp."

The darkness was approaching now, and I grew uneasy that

one such as this would wait stubbornly alone in such discomfort for someone who, in all probability, would never arrive.

"I do not think the one you say you love is coming," I said. "If you sit here in the dark, you will surely freeze to death. Please, light your lamp from mine. Or if, for some reason, mine will not do for you, then, from someone else's. See, out beyond the park railings, many have light. Anyone will be pleased to share their light with you that you might see to make your way home."

"Again, I thank you, but no," she replied. "I await the coming of the Lamplighter."

In my concern for her, I was becoming disturbed now, for she seemed to me inordinately stubborn. "But all light is the same," I insisted. "We all walk by the same light. It is essential you receive light or you will not be able to see and I am willing to share mine with you."

"Not so," she replied. "All light comes from one source, but the lamps of others burn dim and cool. They have barely enough light to see their own way forward. And if they attempt to light mine, their lights will surely go out. Look to your own lamp. See, it is dimming already."

I looked down at my light and I saw that it was so. Its flame burned weakly, the wick short and the fuel dangerously low. I grew uneasy and more irritable. "What is so special about you that you need a better light than the rest of us anyway?" I asked.

She was silent a moment. "I am not special," she replied. "All can light their lamps from the Lamplighter. But many choose not to do so. The one I love is not easily found. Most prefer to light their lamps from one another. They think it easier than seeking the Lamplighter. They convince themselves that it is enough to see their way by the dim light they have. *We will surely make it home*, they say. *We have enough light for the journey*. But for me, this is not so. My path home is steep and rocky. If I do not light my lamp from the Lamplighter, I will not have enough light to see my way clearly to the end of the journey."

As I looked at her, I knew that she spoke the truth. But here was my dilemma. My own light now was growing dimmer by the minute and the darkness was falling. I felt an urge to wait with her for the Lamplighter, for I had begun to have hope he would come. But I was fearful that my lamp would go out before he arrived and I would be left in darkness.

I stood, making ready to leave.

"Will you not wait with me to meet with the Lamplighter?" she asked, her soft voice barely audible in the growing wind. "He will surely be along soon. He always arrives before the darkness falls."

"It's easy for you," I answered roughly in my fear. "You know this Lamplighter. You know him and are confident he will arrive. I have never met him. How can I be sure he will come before darkness falls – if, indeed, he is coming at all? I must be away home before my light fails."

"As you choose," she replied softly. "No one is ever forced to meet the Lamplighter. But one day, perhaps in a lifetime yet to come, I know you will turn and meet with him yourself."

"Pah! What is this nonsense?" I answered, now enraged. "I don't believe there is a Lamplighter. I don't believe there ever was. The light we have is all that we have. It is our destiny to light our lamps from one another. We have no other option than to proceed with the light we have to the end of our journeys. Trust me – I know about these things."

In my anger, I made as if to stride away. But quite suddenly, I stopped, for a question had entered my mind, gripping me with the need to know the answer. "This Lamplighter of yours," I demanded, leaning in towards her in the falling light. "Tell me his name."

As the last of the light slid away she smiled as she answered. "His name," she said, "is Agape. And if you look behind you, you will see his light a little way off through the snow. I promised you he would arrive before the dark. He has been standing there a while now. He is waiting to meet with you."

I turned and stared out into the darkness.

28. A Journey to the Land of Risk

I had intended to be on a book and speaking tour in South East Asia this spring. When on tour, I often teach the value of stretching ourselves beyond the 'Land of Comfort Zone', in order to travel to the 'Land of Risk', in order to unshackle the caged and sleeping poet – the creative energy that lies within. I talk of wild beasts that live in the mountains of that land, beasts of which we may live in great fear. And I speak also of discovering, when we take the risk of making that journey, that those beasts, though they will remain ever wild, love and nurture the Poet inside us, for it is their wildness that is the source of his energy, the secret of his true power.

For reasons beyond my control and that of the organisers of the tour, we had to postpone the trip. I decided, therefore, that I would spend the first three months of the year writing. Indeed, it would be a tremendous opportunity, since I had allocated little concentrated time for writing in perhaps two years.

But when it came to it, I was discomforted to discover that the flow of words, which in years past had gushed so easily, simply would not come. Had I dried out from spending too much time distributing books, in public speaking, and in giving energy? Was the 'Poet Within', whom I am so fond of urging others to access, lost to me forever? At first, I struggled, unwilling to face the presenting reality. I could not accept that the words which are my world, which energise me, and bring insight to others, that these words were simply gone.

I pushed harder, yearning to squeeze out some perceptibly viable literary output in a panicked, fearful thrashing through the dense forest of inner darkness. But the words: still they would not come.

Eventually, I allowed myself to realise that something more fundamental was afoot; that the solution lay elsewhere than in simply trying to be more disciplined, than in taking myself to task and in giving myself a firm talking to for my indolence.

So, I did what I have come to realise is most important to do at times of incongruence, when what I am being is not what I think I should be. I was quiet for a season, waiting for the light to come, the illumination from my inner guides and my outer guides that would reveal where the disconnect lay, or what new revelation awaited the ceasing of my struggles. I read a little, I worked a little – the odd bookshop signing, the occasional fair. Then, quite spontaneously, as it must always happen, synchronicity took control. I came across a book[1] on 'Shadow Work', a personal growth methodology based on Karl Jung's archetype model. The book came to my attention on Facebook, literally moments after a long discussion on the same subject with two gentlemen who bought some of my own books at a signing. The 'coincidence' was too much to ignore. I have long since learned that when confronted with the clanging claxons and flashing lights of synchronicity, I do well to take notice, for something consequential is about to occur.

Shadow work explores the connection between the conscious life we live and the unconscious part of our personality that so fundamentally affects it. To say the least, the book resonated with me. It was clear that a 'next step' was needed. With some considerable trepidation, I booked onto a residential workshop that the author was running. As soon as I did so, something fearful deep inside me began expressing regret and warnings. "Why do this?" it called. "This is going to be difficult and painful. You know you don't want to do this. It's far too much of a risk." My reluctance continued up to, and into, the first night of the programme, when I tossed and turned in sleepless anxiety, angry with myself for risking exposure to this terrifying ordeal.

So, here I was, making once again, the very Journey into the Land of Risk that I so freely advocate to others that they should take. Sure enough, it was on the workshop that I discovered the reason for the sense of imperative I had felt that I should come. It was this: to begin to explore hidden memory that I had been suppressing all my life.

Consider, for a moment, the amount of energy it takes to suppress unwanted and profoundly feared memory for the whole of this lifetime you have so far lived. Imagine the amount of your daily energy you allocate to the part of you that is in charge of keeping you safe. And when you have a sense of the quantum of that energy, then think about what you could do with it once you have decided it is time to turn and face what you need to know to suppress it no longer.

We shall perhaps speak of the detail of the memory I discovered another day. Suffice to say for now though, that the impact of accessing it was monumental. Overwhelmed, I collapsed to the floor with the power of the revelation. I wept and I laughed in a surge of emotion, supported throughout by this remarkable and deeply caring therapist, who is unequalled, in my experience, in personal growth facilitation.

But could such enormous benefit last? I returned home, intrigued to discover what continuing change I might experience. And what a change it was. Here, in the Land of Risk that I had now brought within the boundaries of my own kingdom, the spring sunshine of enlightenment was warming the frozen mountains. And down from those mountains cascaded the snowmelt of awareness, watering a drought-parched land. With the thaw, there also came the wild beasts I had so greatly feared: the roaring lion of Passion, the grizzly bear of Indignation, the identical twins of Tears and Laughter. Relentlessly, they came. They came in determination and they would not stop. For they love the awakening of the Poet and they come to give voice to the creative exposition.

Creativity returned in a way I have not known for perhaps fifteen years. And since then, a week ago now, the revelations have flowed and flowed. The Poet has been unshackled once more and I cannot not make him stop. But there again, why ever would I want him to stop? He is pouring forth his wisdom, his light, in poetry, in metaphorical fiction, both long and short, and in Learnings, like this one. This is why I have travelled once more to the Land of Risk: to unshackle the Poet, or, if you prefer, to make the Zen connection between conscious and unconscious. Awakened, the Poet has snapped the bars of his cage on which he was rattling to get my attention, and he has ripped off its door in the power released by the conscious act of ceasing to suppress memory.

In the words of archetype terminology from the training course, my Magician has paid fealty to my Sovereign, yielding to him the authority that was always rightly his. I really do not mind which metaphor you prefer to use. I am simply satisfied that once again I pour out, in power and lucidity, the energy I have to give because I have been willing to open up to the energy I need to receive.

And my message to you from all of this? Start today, if you are so minded, your own journey to the Land of Risk. Begin to ask yourself what it is you might see, what you might hear, what you might feel, if you open yourself to the energy of love that wants to flow into you, through you and out of you. Consider what might be the possibilities that will open up when you discover how effective you can be. Curiosity, I grant you, did indeed kill the occasional, reckless feline. But indolence and inertia killed inestimably more. Come, take a risk. Change your world and mine, for if you will but see it, you are powerful and you are glorious.[i]

---

[i] Warrior, Magician, Lover, King Rod Boothroyd 978-1722820893

29. Seeking Space

Seek me not in the words
but in the spaces in between;
not in the come go turn-a-day of turning days
but clothed in the cloistered twilight
that shrouds ephemeral voids of softening silence.

Not in the plainsong chiming hour
will you find the nest of plenitude,
nor where gnostic whips unfurl
to curl across the cursed coerced,
inscribed upon Abraxas stones.

I am not found on carousels of power where
Parliaments of rooks and crooks
adjudicate the codicils of Piety,
nor yet within the bustling marketplaces of the garrulous.

Seek me in that somnolent space
– you know it well –
where shimmering shadows meet to
treat and trick the eye
and try the slowing heart to reach for trailing
vines that tremble in the undertow.

You will find me
sitting at the feet of journeys un-commenced
where solitude apprentices her trade
and touchstones mumble half forgiven heresies;
where warriors wield ploughshares
and angels watch while learned
men dance solemnly upon the heads of pins.

Unknowing here shall compensate
the quenchant fires of absolution and
new-birthed immortality unfurled
shall bid the Uninitiate come enter in
this place where endings find beginnings.

30. Inspiration

I was a painter back then. I sought to splash colour on canvas as God paints the summer meadows with the cornflowers and the poppies. I craved reputation, to be ranked among the greatest artists of my generation. In my daydreams, the elders of my town would fall back in amazement at the power of my images. Invitations would be issued to city mayors and burghers, who would come to congratulate me, then humbly plead that I accept their commissions. Nonchalantly, I would add them to the end of my growing waiting list, while the prettiest girls of the Canton vied to become my muses.

But my nights, my nights were not so happy. Alone in my chamber, I feared to extinguish my candle, for in the darkness the terrors would come. And always, the dream was the same. Standing in my studio, with my canvasses stacked around me, I laboured with a burning intensity to create my masterpiece, a Madonna and child, the signature work of my life by which all the world and the generations of time would know my towering greatness.

Then, I would smell the smoke. The fire always started behind me. But so oblivious was I to all but my work, that by the time I recognised it for what it was, it had taken hold. Above me, the ancient oak beams smouldered and cracked, then burst into incandescent flame that rained the fire of heaven down upon my paintings. Too late, I would see my predicament and the impending destruction of my most precious creations. I would grab at the canvas on the easel and the one or two nearest to my feet, only to come to a terrified realisation that I did not know the way out. The roof beams would crash down around me, destroying everything I valued as I sat in the middle of the floor weeping. And just as the heat began to sear the flesh of my hands, I would finally awaken, sweat-soaked, upon my bed.

Last night, the dream was different. Still I laboured at my canvas, still the fire started behind me. But as the roof beams crackled above my head, I took a different course. Without hesitation, I grabbed my largest brush and into the centre of the canvas, I painted a door; an oak-framed door so large it covered the face of the Madonna and all of the child in her arms. I worked rapidly, smoke beginning to fill the studio about me. Once the door in the picture was complete, I seized upon the handle like a madman and turned it, pulling on it with all my strength. It flung itself open with such force that I was thrown back to the floor as a mighty rushing wind blew in, a hurricane so powerful that it extinguished the flames that threatened me. As the wind finally died down, I looked about me, the smoke curling up from my eviscerated canvasses.

This morning, I took all my paintings out behind the studio and made a bonfire of them. My life's work has finally begun.

31. Solstice

There will be a reason stated, it will be known clearly why.
There will be a new unveiling, demonstrations from on high,
There will be a revelation of all truths, yet, by and by.
Jars of honey turned, upended, in the brightest, clearest sky
Will make a new anointing of the hearts that never die.
There will come renewal visions in the moistening of the eye,
A reinvigorated joining, as the freed ones rise and fly,
When we recognise each other, yes, my soulmate,
You and I.

We will stand with one another, look each other in the eye,
And remark upon the wisdom learned in lifetimes now fled by.
You'll be clothed in waves of resonance. With heartstrings you
will tie
Cloths of heaven that I weave you, hemmed with joy that cannot
die,
When below the Tor at Solstice we by Chalice fountains lie.
And we'll hold each other dearly and in joy we'll cry and cry,
For we recognise each other, oh, my soulmate,
You and I.

We will walk together slowly, as the drums and timbrels cry
And, oblivious to others as the dancers pass us by,

We'll vibrate for seven lifetimes as we touch the crystal eye,
As the music-makers celebrate the passing of the lie.
For we need no other presence in the lightening of the sky,
And we need no other joining than our own love,
You and I.

As we walk, the henge will open, our awareness magnify,
And the standing stones will resonate, the goddess glorify.
We will sit on thrones of dignity, and darkness pacify
And marvel at enlightenment that ends the question 'why?'.
For we join as one eternally, my soulmate,
You and I.

I have touched your soul's vibrations, you have always been close
by.
I have felt your constant presence, and on this I most rely:
I will see you, standing in the light, when next I choose to die.
In this lifetime – or the next one –
I will meet you in the sky.

32. Make Like a Tree

I helped old friends with a house removal this week. By the time I arrived, the internal packing was complete, but there remained much to move outdoors. As we dismantled garden furniture, loaded planters and hosepipes, bins and ornaments, I kept to myself what I began to realise: that much of what was being removed to the new address would in all likelihood not be used again and might not even be reassembled. It reminded me of the time, years back now, when I, too, went through this process of sifting through a lifetime's acquisitions, in my case dismantling a family home after 25 years of marriage. As my downsize was to be dramatic, an enormous amount ended up on the skip (there was no eBay at that time, and recycling centres were a mere twinkle in the conservationist's eye).

As our life journey moves on, how reluctant we can be to relinquish that to which we have a long attachment. We are apt to externalise into our possessions our sense of identity, in an attempt, unconscious or otherwise, to preserve our continuity and shore up the dilapidating boundaries of our soul. Once we have invested our energy, our sense of identity in this way, the release of these transient items to which we have imputed so much worth becomes difficult for us and often intensely painful. "How can I live without my books, my vinyl records, my collection of thimbles, my … [insert your own preferred delusion here]?"

Yet, if we do, when years later, something happens to spark recollection, we are often apt to smile and say, "Why ever was I so bothered about losing that old thing?" Our energy, our focus, our definition of what matters, has moved on.

As the work proceeded and we moved possessions from the back garden to the front drive, my eye was caught by an awe-inspiring magnolia tree on the front lawn, which was in the process of shedding its superb blossom. Many blossoms remained on the tree, but far more lay on the ground beneath it, no longer useful, discarded. In seeing such a spectacle, we find ourselves saddened. We want to cling on to the beauty we see disappearing, for we love the beautiful, do we not? "Pick them up, they are gorgeous," we want to say to the tree. "They glorify the world. They must be preserved." In the confrontation of endings, in the perception of loss, there can be much sadness.

But the magnolia has an answer for us. "Why ever would I want to keep them?" she asks. "Their time is past. If I hold on to them, there can be no growth, and you will soon see me adorned, not with beauty, but decay."

Later, I was talking to the wife of the couple moving home, a friend of some twenty years standing. Without my telling her what I had been thinking, she referred to the tree in our conversation. It is a tree that she has greatly valued and enjoyed during their period of occupancy of the house. "Yesterday, as we were packing," she said, "I stopped a while to watch the magnolia through the window. When the wind blew, it was quite uncanny, like a little localised hurricane swirling around it, when all else in the garden was calm. The tree shook off its blooms as if it were talking to us, saying, 'Time to go, time to go. I don't mind that you're moving on. I salute you in our parting. I shower my glory for you in an extravagant farewell.'" And then, my friend's focus changed. "Much that we're taking with us," she said wistfully, "We'll never use it again. It should really be dumped or recycled." And then, she reminded me of why she did not do so. "But my husband has dementia. He won't throw anything away. I have no right to throw out stuff if he's still attached to it." I was taken aback. Saddened and a little chastened for my speedy judgement. Her integrity had confounded my inauthenticity.

All pain, say my Buddhist friends, emanates from attachment. I have long sought to act in keeping with this knowledge, parting with objects often, acquiring few – and these only when really needed. It has, by contrast, been much harder to release old states, old preferences, old preoccupations with the opinions that I think others hold of me. For these have been the markers of my identity. It is with these that I have staked my claim upon the external world. Yet, I also know that it is when I am willing to release my tenuous grip that I release also the constraints they place upon me, enabling me to move ever onward, ever further inward, where the real prize lies.

All those years ago, when I left my family home, I hugged many of the tall Scots Pines that ringed the gardens, towering in silent majesty over the crumbling edifices of human existence – the house, the outbuildings, the possessions now consigned to the skip. A year later, I passed by that house again. The new owner, with his different map of the world, his different understanding of value, had felled every one of them. I felt great pain – perhaps that of the trees, certainly my own.

When, around the same time, I wrote *Forest Rain*, my first book of Learnings, I used the following sentences: "The only possession we carry with us beyond the grave is our learning. The only substance in the universe we cannot replicate is spirit."

Take great care over the baggage you choose to accumulate, be it physical or metaphysical. It can be replaced – if you want to, if you really need to. But do you want to? Do you really need to? When the hurricane blows, open your hands and let the blossom waft away. In the words of the old pun, when it's time to move on, make like a tree and leave.

If you have benefited from reading *Forest Dawn*, would you please review it at Amazon. This will help others to find and enjoy the book.

On Amazon.co.uk, type: Michael Forester Forest Dawn

A big

Thank you!

For buying a book by Michael Forester.

This voucher entitles you to a

second purchase

of any different book at a

40% discount

Simply make your selection from http://michaelforester.co.uk/books

At the check out page apply the coupon **second book** . Michael Forester will forward a signed copy of your purchase to you directly, dedicated in the wording of your choice.

Forest Rain
Spiritual Learnings for a New Age

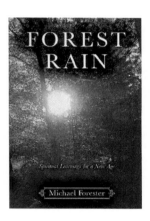

"Seek me, not in the words, but in the spaces in between." This unique collection of essays, metaphors and verse has been called one of the great books of all time, a book that will open doors in your heart and mind.

- The soul awakening that follows a near death experience
- The unseen protectors who are always about us, guiding our life journey
- The love we pursue relentlessly until we realise that it was always seeking us
- The high places of the heart where we see across death and into eternity
- The heart-rending lessons learned on the death of a marriage
- The power that tears hold to heal the pain of loss

- The married couple, so at war with each other, that their resentment takes on human form
- The simple honesty of a son as he faces the impending death of his father
- The man who found his soul in a broken mirror

Forest Rain will lead you on a journey into your own soul, to face your fears and regrets, and thus access the healing that leads to the love that has always awaited you.

Author signed copies of this book can be obtained from **www.michaelforester.co.uk/books**

One Journey
A Travelogue of Awakening

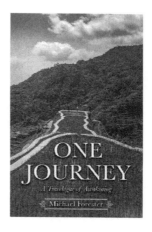

We commence our journey on the journey the moment we enter the physical world and complete it the moment we leave. The journey is travelled on a road of self-discovery.

Here are four voyages on that road, undertaken over a period of fourteen years:

- In the Amazon Rain Forest, a confrontation with the unceasing exploitation of its resources and people.

- In South Africa, an encounter with the power of forgiveness, fifteen years after the ending of apartheid.

- In Nepal and the Himalayas, a pilgrimage of self-discovery.

- In the Philippines, an exploration the impact of economic modernisation upon the people and the land.   Each explores how, if we have the eyes to see and the ears to hear, our voyages into the world are, in reality, a reflection of our Journey into ourselves.

Author signed copies of this book can be obtained from http://www.michaelforester.co.uk/books

If It Wasn't For That Dog

*It's amazing what you can achieve with persistence, a
bit of chopped liver and a second-hand teddy bear...*

It's amazing what you can achieve with persistence, a bit of
chopped liver and a second hand teddy bear...

New Forest Author, Michael, began losing his hearing at the age
of 30, due to a genetic condition. By the time he was 46, his
hearing was all but gone and he was ready to try anything that
might help. Then someone suggested that getting a dog might be
a good idea - not just any dog, but a hearing dog from Hearing
Dogs for Deaf People. And when, two years later, he was
presented with a hearing dog of his own called Matt, Michael just
knew life would be so much easier.

Amazing how wrong you can be, isn't it!

If It Wasn't For That Dog is the story of Matt's first year with
Michael, the challenges and accomplishments of climbing the
Hearing Dog learning curve, the profound changes he stimulated

and the inestimable joy he confers magically on everyone who meets him. But most of all, it is the story of the strange power of meaty treats to work miracles in doggy behaviour.

Author signed copies of this book can be obtained from http://www.michaelforester.co.uk/books

Dragonsong

Sometimes Nothing but the Death of Your Father Will Do

Rebekah, noblewoman of Albion, has been driven to madness by the murder of her lover Vidar. In her torment she bargains with the Prince of Demons to turn her into a dragon. Thus transformed, she seeks to take revenge upon her father, Merlin, whom she is fooled into believing is responsible for Vidar's death. To save the world from the ravages of Dragonsong, Merlin is forced to banish his beloved daughter to Hell, regardless of the consequences for him personally. Behind the subterfuge stands Oberon, Captain-King of Elves. He does not foresee the devastation his jealousy and unrequited love for Rebekah will unleash upon Gaia when he frees her from Merlin's spell and summons her from Hell to support his war against Albion. To save Gaia a second time, Merlin is forced to travel back in time to prepare a warrior capable of overcoming the dragon through the power of the Sleep Stone. But he does not foresee the bond that will develop between the dragon and his own assistant, the

Seer, Michael of Albion. If Lady Attie and Michael prove unable to return the Sleep Stone to the mouth of Hell in time, the Demon Army will be swarm out of Hell and overrun Gaia. Time. Time is the key. Time is the only solution to Gaia's destiny – but only if the gods of Asgard can find a way to stop it.

The Goblin Child

And other stories

Well, hello there. Why don't you step inside and take a look round? You remember this place, don't you? That's right. You've been here before. And us. Surely you remember us. We're old friends. This is where the light in your eyes glimpses the darkness in your mind. Sit down and stay a while – if you can face the risk of finding out who you really are, that is. I'll introduce you to some friends of mine:

Meet the man who remembers his birth. He wishes he didn't.

And the goblin child – if his mother is to be believed.

Or how about the boy who takes his god to school?

Here's Madeleine, the author who can't get beyond chapter seven – because of the raven with white eyes, that is.

And Santa. Yes, you really must meet Santa.

But really it's all about David, who spent his life circling the moon – just like you and I do, in fact

Come with me. Come with me now.

Author signed copies of this book can be obtained from
http://www.michaelforester.co.uk/books

A Home For Other Gods

Everything is under control

It's 2117.

A country where everything you do has to be approved by the State; a State that tells you what to eat, when to shower, when to make love, what to think.

As the waters start to rise in the city, the fish people begin to arrive. Ultimately compliant, obedient without question, they open and close their mouths incessantly, saying nothing.

When Greg dares to think for himself, the Departmental Republic seeks to draw him into their elite to keep him quiet, to force his compliance. But if he agrees to be elevated to the level of the shadowy 'Gods,' it's going to cost him his home and the life of his family.

People are saying this ground-breaking novella reads like a follow-on to 1984.

Author signed copies of this book can be obtained from **http://www.michaelforester.co.uk/books**

Vicious

A novel of punk rock and the second coming

For thirty years, Tolly's been waiting for the reincarnation of rock star Sid Vicious who's definitely coming back to love her forever. Now that she's certain she's found him in the form of young Henry, well, Henry's girlfriend Laura has to be stalked and eliminated, doesn't she?

But… something's not right. Because when Tolly kidnaps Laura, hovering in the background are unearthly wispy creatures – *Ethereals*, they call themselves. And what's more they seem to be subject to a series of rules. Is this some kind of a game? Could Laura really be miraculously pregnant with the second coming, as Pastor Littlemann insists? Or is she just as insane as Tolly?

Vicious is a cracking good read, guaranteed have you guessing right up to the final pages as to what's really going on. If you like the novels of Stephen King you'll love this book!

A must-read for anyone who loves an intriguing mystery.

Author signed copies of this book can be obtained from
http://www.michaelforester.co.uk/books

Biographical

Michael Forester is a deafened author who lives between the New Forest and the sea. He is a full time author and public speaker, travelling both in the UK and internationally, speaking inspirationally and signing his books for readers in locations as far apart as the UK, Thailand, Cambodia and the Philippines. He is the author of ten published books to date, on subjects as diverse as business strategy, spiritual inspiration and epic fantasy poetry.

Michael's own journey has taken him from early years in academia into middle years in management training and Neuro Linguistic Programming. It has taken him from normal hearing to near-profound deafness and the life-changing arrival of a hearing dog, Matt. It has taken him through a miraculously survived suicide attempt in 2002, into a spiritual awakening.

He has travelled to over forty countries, from the Amazon Rainforest, encountering ecological devastation, to South Africa, experiencing post-Apartheid forgiveness; from a personal pilgrimage in search of the singing bowls of Nepal, to a first-hand examination of the darker side of economic modernisation in the Philippines, besides many other destinations.

For speaking engagements and further information he can be contacted at **michaelforesterauthor@gmail.com**

Printed in Poland
by Amazon Fulfillment
Poland Sp. z o.o., Wrocław

57899503R00094